BACKPACKING IN ALPS AND PYRENEES

BACKPACKING
IN ALPS AND PYRENEES

by

SHOWELL STYLES

LONDON
VICTOR GOLLANCZ LTD
1976

ISBN 0 575 02131 2

PRINTED IN GREAT BRITAIN
BY EBENEZER BAYLIS AND SON LTD
THE TRINITY PRESS, WORCESTER, AND LONDON

Dedicated to
Colin Vaughan Morgan,
good companion on these and other
backpacking journeys

Contents

Illustrations

1*

Second morning at "Camp One": Grand Combin, Petit Combin and Val de Bagnes (*photo Colin V. Morgan*)

Descent from Col de Sorebois (9,269 feet): Weisshorn, Lo Besso, Zinal Rothhorn (*photo Colin V. Morgan*)

Campsite on the Täschalp (*photo Colin V. Morgan*)

Looking back at the Simeli Pass (9,916 feet) from the path to the Bistinen (*photo Colin V. Morgan*)

On the path from the Hannig Pass to Saas Fee showing the Weissmies (*photo Colin V. Morgan*)

The Bernese Oberland seen across the Rhone Valley from the last mountain camp at 8,100 feet (*photo Colin V. Morgan*)

DIAGRAM ROUTE MAPS

Foreword on Backpacking

A definition may be needed. The Concise Oxford English Dictionary, 1974 edition, has no mention of *backpacker* or *backpacking* or the verb *to backpack*, though all three—and the sport itself—have been used and practised in Britain for the past five years at least. In that period no less than three handbooks to the craft of backpacking have been published. One of these I wrote myself, and gave my own definition of the practitioner: "You are a Backpacker when you set out on a journey carrying on your back everything you need for existence —bed and shelter, food and the means of cooking it, and the minimum extra comforts you consider necessary to the happy life."

The phenomenal growth of backpacking as a way of holiday living is an end-product of the British Walking Revolution which has taken place during the last half-century. Side by side with the virtual closing of the Queen's Highway to foot passengers, a reopening and linking of the old walking tracks made possible a new form of walking-tour, the Long-Distance Footpath. There are now 1,500 miles of such footpaths in England and Wales and every year more mileage on the moorlands and open country is being dedicated to the hardy walker; but the resurgence of pedestrianism has been too sudden and widespread for these facilities. Already some stretches of the most popular footpath, the 250-mile Pennine Way, have had to be closed and bypassed to give them a chance of recovery from the erosion of over-usage. Guidebooks and open-air magazines have hitherto emphasised British backpacking routes to the exclusion of the almost illimitable opportunities beyond the Channel, and it is time to take a look at some of the magnificent journeys by which any active man or woman willing to assume the pilgrim insignia of pack and staff can come to close quarters with the finest scenery in Europe. This book, describing two long journeys in the Alps and one in the Spanish Pyrenees, may serve as an introduction to European backpacking.

This kind of travel is nothing new, of course.

> Jog on, jog on the footpath way
> And merrily hent the stile-a

was the way of the majority of mankind before the advent of the motor-car, and the backpacker merely follows by choice a mode of journeying which innumerable adventurers of the past followed of necessity. True, the main routes through the more scenic parts of Europe have been appropriated by the motoring tourist, but the new and overcrowded roads have canalised the human traffic and left the vast and lovely areas on either hand freer and wilder than they were before, particularly in the mountains of Europe. Here, between the petrol fumes of the valleys and the snow and ice where only the climber can go, is a much wider region crossed by little-used tracks, sometimes linked by pathless or sparsely waymarked stretches, through which a backpacker may travel the length of a great mountain range or even pass from country to country. And in his two or three weeks of free wandering he will see far more of his chosen corner of Earth than the car-driver or the climber.

I have described the three routes followed in 1972, 1973, and 1974 in detail, with "the particular accidents gone by", so that the reader will have some idea of the conditions, pleasures, and pains of this kind of backpacking. Those who may be moved to follow along these or similar routes will find precise information about equipment, maps, and itineraries in the Appendices.

S.S.

BACKPACKING IN ALPS AND PYRENEES

ONE

The Bernese Oberland

1. BEX TO GSTEIG

Bex. Tram to Fontannaz-Seulaz, thence on foot. Col des Essets (6,690'). Pas de Cheville (6,723'). Lac de Derborence. Col de la Fava (7,639'). Col du Sanetsch (7,330'). Gsteig. 3½ days, 3 camps.

There is just one moment when carrying a thirty-pound pack is purest pleasure unalloyed: the moment when you first shoulder the pack after twenty-four hours of hoicking it on and off ships and in and out of trains. This moment dawned on Colin and me in the early afternoon of July 28th at a tramway halt in the forest above Bex; dawned, and very quickly faded. Five minutes on the sunlit track through the trees was enough to impress on us the weight of the burdens we were to carry for three weeks and over fifteen passes, from end to end of the long Oberland range.

"Montreux to Meiringen on foot" has a fine alliterative ring, but even a flagellant would shy at humping a heavy load two thousand feet uphill through the villa-streets of Montreux in the interests of purism. Our aim was to walk the length of the Oberland by its mountain paths, and there was no pilgrim vow to prevent us from using public transport to get us to the start of those paths. So we had stayed on the train for four stations beyond Montreux and disembarked at Bex in steamy-hot sunshine. The little electric tram that bore us quickly out of the town was equipped for climbing. Confronted by an abrupt steepening of the road, it lowered a cogwheel from its innards with a groan and became a Mountain Railway, curling up the shelves of forest that rise above the Avançon glen. We got out at a place with a name like a fanfare— Fontannaz-Seulaz; it was a forest clearing with nothing in sight but the trees, the railway line, and a pile of hewn logs. A

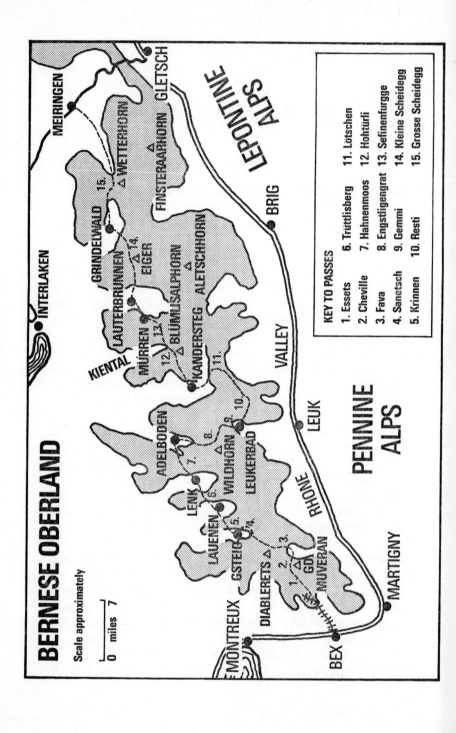

BERNESE OBERLAND

Scale approximately

0 miles 7

INTERLAKEN

MEIRINGEN

GLETSCH

WETTERHORN

GRINDELWALD 15.

FINSTERAARHORN

14.
EIGER

LAUTERBRUNNEN

BLÜMLISALPHORN

ALETSCHHORN

13.
MÜRREN

KIENTAL

12.

KANDERSTEG

11.

BRIG

LEPONTINE
ALPS

VALLEY

10.

ADELBODEN

LEUK

9.
WILDHORN
8.
LEUKERBAD

RHONE

LENK
7.
6.

PENNINE
ALPS

LAUENEN 5.

GSTEIG 4.

3.

DIABLERETS

2.

1. GD
MUVERAN

MONTREUX

MARTIGNY

BEX

KEY TO PASSES

1. Essets	6. Truttlisberg	11. Lötschen
2. Cheville	7. Hahnenmoos	12. Hohtürli
3. Fava	8. Engstligengrat	13. Sefinenfurgge
4. Sanetsch	9. Gemmi	14. Kleine Scheidegg
5. Krinnen	10. Resti	15. Grosse Scheidegg

stony path branched off through the bushes and we took the first steps of the 200-mile walk, having first (at Colin's suggestion) cut a couple of stout staffs from a thicket.

I must briefly introduce Colin, a shortish, indestructible South Walian with an irrepressible twinkle and an inexhaustible energy. His knowledge of Grand Opera is encyclopaedic and when happy he rends the air with arias in *tenore robusto*. My Alpine climbing days are over, but Colin had been climbing in the Valais during the previous summer, hurtling up and down the Dom and the Zinal Rothhorn and the rest until even he had had enough. As a consequence, he proposed to spend this season in a less energetic form of mountaineering and at the same time see more of Swiss mountain scenery. The second part of this proposition more than fulfilled expectation; the first part proved illusory. But at the end of the journey (it took us twenty-three days in all) we were both convinced that long-distance backpacking through the Alps, living rough and camping high when possible, is by far the best way of taking all that Switzerland has to offer to an ordinarily active man or woman.

What we carried in our packs is listed in Appendix C. To guide us we had the maps of the Swiss Landeskarte, 1:50000, and a note or two in the back of my Log from Muirhead's *Switzerland*. From these we had deduced that the first two or three days of the journey, penetrating the western end of the Bernese Oberland, were likely to be a tame plodding along easy paths through mild foothill scenery. True, Muirhead spoke of "the impressive gorge of the upper Avançon" above which we must pass, but the map suggested to us a sub-Alpine lack of excitement. We could hardly have been more mistaken.

For the first hour or so, indeed, expectation was justified. The stony path debouched on a motorable lane in the valley. It was very, very hot. We sweated past the hamlet of Les Plans and took a side path marked "Pont de Nant par l'Échelle" where two rocky rises were passed by wooden ladders. Trees obscured all view of the deep ravine on our right. *"Impressive gorge of upper Avançon invisible in forest, so sucks to Muirhead,"* comments my Log. Then, quite suddenly, the path emerged into an upper glen walled by enormous crags. Horns of rock, snow-powdered, jutted three thousand feet overhead. In front the track climbed along a rocky flank embroidered with alpine flowers to cross a waterfall tumbling out of a cleft. With a sense of release—and of relief, for we had been going for four hours—we started to look out for a camp-site. Except for the four-foot width of the track there seemed to be no flat space anywhere on the slopes in the valley-head, but when we had crossed the little stone bridge over the waterfall ravine we found a charming site on a grassy ledge overlooking the glen we had ascended. A minor rock-climb was necessary in order to fill the folding plastic bucket from the stream; otherwise the mountains, as always, provided such comforts as flat rocks for table and seats and a sheltered nook for the stove.

There is always a special emotion, a mingling of anticipation and apprehension, about the pitching of the first camp on a long backpacking journey. Will the equipment, necessarily reduced to a minimum, prove to be too minimal? Did we bring matches and a can-opener? Shall we be able to eat the extremely basic food that is to be our diet for the next three weeks? Apprehension faded as the single-pole Itisa Senior—roomiest of light-weight tents and quickest to erect—sat happily on the ledge and the propane-gas stove hissed under the billy. Potato mash, Oxo, fruit salad were well enough, but only later on when a full day's march added the best of sauces to such meals were they to acquire the true ambrosial flavour.

Light thickened as the after-supper pipes were smoked. Tobacco-smoke curled against a background of cloud creeping down the darkening crags. It was very still in that upland place. By nine o'clock we were in our sleeping-bags.

The Bernese Alps fray out at their western end into deep valleys and separated masses above the Rhone Valley where it widens to hold the Lake of Geneva, but the main ridge of high peaks is still discernible, ending in the Grand Muveran (10,043 feet), whose cloud-capped precipices were close above our first camp-site. For the backpacking traverse of the range we planned to keep as close as possible to the main ridge, crossing it more than once but holding always to routes where the staff and not the ice-axe was the traveller's implement. This meant crossing the passes over the side-ribs of the main ridge, particularly on the northern flank. Our flying start from Bex, avoiding the road pass over the Col de Pillon, now confronted us with two passes close together, the Col des Essets and the Pas de Cheville, both under 7,000 feet. They crossed branch ridges on the south side of the range. Beyond them we hoped to traverse into the Col du Sanetsch (7,330 feet) and cross the range to Gsteig on the north flank. Between Cheville and Sanetsch, however, was a high section where the map showed no pass and about which Muirhead had nothing to say; we relied on our not inconsiderable mountaincraft to get us across this section. The distance to Gsteig was not great and I had estimated with confidence that we could do it with two camps on the way. It was our first trip of this kind and I had a lot to learn.

"It's for heat," declared the always optimistic Colin when he saw the low clouds next morning; this was to become the motto of our journey.

Breakfast of boiled egg, bread-and-butter and tea was standard. We were away at ten past nine up the path, zig-zagging above the glen into a huge upland pasture surrounded by mountains and full of beautiful Simmental cows. The path, hitherto plain, was indistinguishable here, but the simplest of map-reading kept us on course. Amid a jangling of cow-bells, which the mountain-faces echoed, we crossed the mile-wide pasture and regained the path on the easy ascent to the Col des Essets. The day was cloudy-bright and cool, its freshness offsetting the chafe of rucksack-straps on unaccustomed shoulders. The flowers helped, too—unending drifts of trumpet gentian, yellow arnica and blue campanulas; there had been alpenrose in the glen lower down.

The grassy saddle of the Col des Essets discharged us down-hill on to the slopes above the chalets of Anzeindaz. For the first time we came upon other walkers here; a motorable road had just reached Anzeindaz and half-a-dozen motor-borne tourists were stretching their legs to see the view from the Pas de Cheville. We followed, and found the view worth their effort and ours. Though the pass itself is not very exciting it commands the singularly picturesque hollow of Derborence, an almost totally enclosed valley where the snow cornices of the Diablerets overhang a blue lake in green forests five thousand feet below. None of the tourists followed us on the descent, which was a scenic affair of well-planned zigzags below crags and overhangs,

nowhere difficult but more interesting than we had expected
from the map.

A lane passable by cars has reached the Lac de Derborence
and its wild beauty is now, inevitably, soiled. A jerry-built
café where our path joined the road dispensed wine and
biscuits, but when I tried to buy bread and tobacco (already
foreseeing an extra night out before Gsteig), they had none.
We had made eight hours' going and were tired, so we
marched a little way along the lake and camped in the trees
above it.

"We'll make Gsteig tomorrow," said Colin as we smoked
bedtime pipes. "Did you see the signpost at the café?"

I had seen it, a new yellow sign saying *Col du Sanetsch 4 heures.
Passage Difficile.* Just how *difficile*, I wondered? Next morning
we were to find out.

It was a still and clouded morning, but Colin's "It's for heat"
was only too accurate a prophecy. By the time we had clambered across the Éboulement des Diablerets (as the map calls
the gigantic slope of débris west of the lake) our open shirts
were clinging wetly to our chests and a brilliant sun was
pouring its heat into the rock-walled basin of Derborence. The
clambering was unnecessary. We were traversing high in an
attempt to avoid using the motorable lane, but in the end we
had to drop down on to it and accept its zigzag progress up the
steeps below the Diablerets precipice. This precipice was part
of a continuous semicircle of enormous cliffs which appeared
to close in the northern side of the bowl entirely. We had been
unable to spot any exit route that would be practicable without
a climbing-rope, yet up those cliffs we must somehow get to
reach the Col du Sanetsch. In one place only was there the
semblance of a break: a torrent, the Lizerne, came down a
narrow gorge at the base of the cliffs to our right and above it
the verticalities looked shorter. But there was no discernible
way out of the gorge. Indeed, the waymarks we were following
appeared to lead directly up to the face of the Diablerets.

As far as Derborence we had seen none of the painted
waymarks of which the Swiss are so fond. The route we took
could be followed by anyone with the veriest rudiments of
map-reading and we hadn't put a foot wrong. Now, on the
zigzag lane, we had red-and-white waymarks to guide us and

the first thing we did was to miss the route. In the Oberland yellow waymarks indicate a path suitable for active tourists; red-and-white marks mean a mountaineer's route. Our marks, at longish intervals, had not been seen for some time and the lane—now a narrow track—was trending leftward away from our course when we met an aged peasant and stopped to ask the way. My halting French produced results. With much gesticulation we were bidden back down the track to where a tiny path diverged to enter the gorge. And here were the waymarks once more.

I say "tiny" advisedly. In one place, where it rounded a near-vertical corner above the ravine, the path was just wide enough to take a bootsole. The heavy sack scraped along the rock on the left, the torrent roared black in its bed fifty sheer feet below on the right. Good balance was life. And it was oven-like, the heat in the gorge. We climbed panting to a red-and-white waymark at the foot of a long scree of round stones. The scree mounted to the base of a huge wall of rock, absolutely perpendicular, a place for pitons and étriers if ever there was one. But the glacis of stones, scorching hot to the hands, edged us leftward until with dramatic suddenness a cleft like a giant lift-shaft opened in the rock-wall and we could rest, panting, in the cool shade of its cavernous base.

This cleft of the Lizerne is very like the Devil's Kitchen in North Wales but much easier to climb—Easy Moderate, perhaps, but exposed. Boulders wedged in the bottom of the shaft lead upwards until one can traverse out, on good holds, across the left-hand wall to a ledge. Above this a short vertical chimney provided with a fixed wire rope for handholds ends on easy ground at the top.

"Dicey," commented Colin, watching my struggles on the last six feet.

It certainly felt "dicey" with a two-stone pack on one's shoulders. A slip, and you'd be on the scree 200 feet below. But if we'd had the ten-metre perlon line we later bought, it needn't have been dicey at all; and—for this and other uses— I commend this bit of equipment to anyone who follows the Oberland Way.

Above the rock-wall we found easy terrain of grassy alps and sparkling streams where, since it was well past noon, we lunched on hard-boiled eggs and black-cherry jam. Then, very slowly because of leg-muscles not yet hardened to their task, we toiled up a meandering track to the crest of our third pass, 7,639 feet. This Col de la Fava (nameless on the map) is a notch at the right-angled corner between the long north-south ridge of Mont Gond and the longer massif of peaks and glaciers called the Diablerets. Standing as it were on the jutting point of the corner we had on our left front the white slope of the Tsanfleuron Glacier descending from the Diablerets, to our right and far below the wide green trough of the Tsanfleuron valley sweeping down to the invisible Rhone, and in front the rock and snow peaks of the main Oberland range with the gap of the Col du Sanetsch opening between blunt Sanetschhorn and sharp Arpelistock. The Sanetsch pass was a mere two miles from where we stood. But between us and it was fixed, not a great gulf, but a phenomenon nearly as forbidding: an immense contorted waste of limestone that had once been the bed of the glacier. Innumerable clefts opened all across its angled surface and they were clefts twenty feet deep. Gsteig and its fleshpots was only three or four miles beyond the Sanetsch, but to launch out across that chaotic terrain in late afternoon, with the skies beginning to darken with storm-clouds, was plainly foolish.

Our waymarked route knew better, too. The red-and-white marks led up and down across the rocks for a few minutes and then dived sharply down to the right, following a gully where pink androsacae gleamed in the niches of the limestone walls. An hour later we were pitching the tent on a patch of turf sprinkled with gentians; and not a minute too soon. The hailstorm broke as we were closing the tent door, and when it had passed, the little torrent that hurried down past our site was chocolate-brown with mud. Colin had prudently carried a flask of water over the col and we were able to cook soup from a packet and brew tea, making with the last of our biscuits a somewhat frugal meal. From this camp at 6,600 feet we looked up at the Diablerets snowfields pallid in the dusk; their chill breath flowing down the tilted desert of limestone made a sleeping-bag in a candle-lit tent a very desirable place to be. Wrapped with every bit of clothing we possessed, we dowsed the candle and were asleep by eight o'clock.

Next morning we ended the first stage of our journey by arriving at the pleasant village of Gsteig.

It was a fine morning but a disappointing start, for we came at once to a motorable road (though there were no cars on it) running up to the pass from the direction of the Rhone valley. The Col du Sanetsch is an ancient pass, in use since the Middle Ages, and it could be expected that the automobile would thrust its way over here as it has too often done elsewhere. So we thought, resignedly. And—as happens very infrequently— resignation had its reward. For the road ran only to the dam of a small reservoir lake on the pass, and on the col with its wooden cross we looked from the lip of a roadless precipice to the green and sunlit floor of the Saane valley 4,000 feet below, with Gsteig village like a toy model in the middle of it. A tremendous ravine with the Sanetschschuss leaping and roaring in it cleft the precipice, and by the old and stony mule-track cut into the side of the ravine we came down to flat meadows where brown smiling folk were haymaking.

Ravine, mule-track, and haymakers were all idyllic; but three hours' going on the ghost of a breakfast leaves one with little stomach for idylls. All morning we had talked inter- mittently of our depleted stores and the coming replenishment, and the repetition of "tobacco, bread, sugar, wine" had become a sort of litany corresponding to the Buddhist pilgrim's *Om mane padme hum*. On the flower-spangled path between the wooden chalets I contrived to put on speed. And by the time Colin limped into Gsteig I was sitting at a table outside the Bear Inn with bread-and-cheese and red wine for two in front of me.

2. GSTEIG TO ADELBODEN

Gsteig. Krinnen Pass (5,446'). Trüttlisberg Pass (6,686'). Hahnenmoos Pass (6,410'). 3 days, 4 camps including off-day camp at Adelboden.

For the mature backpacker, an official camping site is to a "wild" site as tinned strawberries are to the fresh-picked fruit. We had resolved to use the organised site facilities of Switzerland only if we had to, for though the intensive cultivation in the valleys makes field camping difficult, the mountainsides above the upper chalets provide pleasanter sites—and purer water. The Swiss National Tourist Office in London supplies a list of such official sites, and Gsteig was one of the eight places on our route which boasted accommodation for campers. Dallying over lunch and making the round of Gsteig's three foodstuff shops to stock up for another three days brought the afternoon to four o'clock, which gave too little time for climbing out of the village to a camp-site on the way to our next pass, so we made for the "Heiti" site, a quarter of a mile uphill on the Col du Pillon road. The darkening afternoon justified this decision by sending down a heavy shower five minutes after the tent was pitched.

The official site was the grass verge of a lane and inclined to be muddy. Dormobiles and caravans occupied most of it but we had another tent for neighbour, its occupants a Scottish student and his girl-friend on a hitch-hiking tour. Colin presented the Scot with the book he had brought with him to read in spare moments, Dickens's *Christmas Books*; a gesture which may have had something to do with the facts that the book was heavy and that we were unlikely to have many spare moments. The camp Warden came round collecting fees (the equivalent of 50p. for a night) and then we dined, on *rösti* and meat hash, fruit salad, and a bottle of *rosé* which cost about thirty pence. *Rösti* is a tinned food common throughout Switzerland, a potato-and-soya base which mixes well with all kinds of meat and is guaranteed to satisfy the gourmand if not the gourmet. Neither *rösti*-hash nor heavy rain prevented us from sleeping soundly that night; and in the sunshine of next morning, after delaying for an hour to dry out the tent on a roadside fence, we were away for our fifth and lowest pass, the Krinnen.

In crossing the Col du Sanetsch we had passed from the south to the north flank of the Oberland chain. On our right hand now as we travelled eastward were the peaks of the Wildhorn and Wildstrubel and their subsidiaries, and over three northern-reaching ridges of these mountains we had to scramble to reach Adelboden. Krinnen, Trüttlisberg, and Hahnenmoos are the passes across these ridges and all of them are low and easy. After the Col de la Fava they seemed very

tame, though pretty enough in a conventional flowers-and-trees
sort of way. Another thing they had in common, and by which
I chiefly remember them, was mud.

A yellow *Wanderweg* signpost in the centre of the village
pointed the way to the Krinnen Pass, and this is the wrong
way to take because the waymarking peters out among steep
hayfields and leaves you stranded on the wrong side of a
valley. We had to traverse sodden hillsides sloping at 45° to
get on the proper path, which you start by going a quarter of a
mile north along the road from Gsteig and turning right at
another yellow sign. The proper path was indescribably
muddy. Mud—there's nothing quite like it for heating the
blood when you have to climb 3,000 feet of it with a heavy
pack. The trouble was that the Krinnen crossing never gets
higher than the treeline, and the path mounts across hillsides
anciently cleared and cultivated. Lunch, a short way below
the summit (5,446 feet), was an oasis in a tilted desert of mud,
a little ridge of pines where there were wild strawberries to
eat with the half mug of *rosé* from Colin's flask and unidentifiable butterflies decorating the asters and yellow arnicas.

The descent was pastorally beautiful as well as muddy, but
because of the cloud and haze we had no views of the Oberland
snows. During all this day and the next the glaciers and
snow-crests of the Wildhorn that hung close above us were
invisible in dense low vapours which Colin asserted were
"for heat" but to my mind suggested more rain to come. We
came down into Lauenen at half past two. A charming village
this, quieter than Gsteig because there's no through road, and—
as we saw when we looked down on it from our camp that
evening—with impressive peaks and a fine waterfall at the head
of its valley. The shop where we topped-up our stores was hung
about with Swiss national flags, as were most of the houses; for
this was Swiss National Day, August 1st, and as we started out
on the Trüttlisberg path a firework or two banged a salute.
It was a broad plain path, waymarked in yellow as well,
climbing steadily past terraced fields and perched chalets and
at last steepening to zigzag through pine-forest. Turning aside
here, up the course of a torrent, we found what my Log calls
"a delightful spot, infinitely preferable to organised site". It was in
fact rather damp and lush with vegetation, but it was remote

enough for an all-over wash in the torrent (perishing cold but needed) followed by a stentorian rendering of a *Tosca* aria by Colin; among the disadvantages of organised camp-sites are the necessity of being respectably clothed in camp and the restraint required of operatic enthusiasts. When we looked out of the tent that night, after supper and wine and cigar, we could see the mountain-top bonfires reddening the low clouds beyond the dark trough of the Lauenen valley.

Perhaps because the earth beneath us was thoroughly sodden, we had a cold night here at 4,800 feet. It hadn't rained, though, so we could pack up a dry tent and get away at 8.45 in cloudy-bright weather. The time we'd spent grubbing the mud from our vibram soles had been wasted, for the 1,800 feet of ascent was all as soft as Gloucestershire ploughland, with the path marked by stakes painted red-and-white and stuck in the slope. (I don't know why the *Bergweg* colours were used here.) It ended on a grassy col from which bald ridges rose into the clouds on either hand. At 6,686 feet we were above the treeline on the Trüttlisberg, and—as on the Krinnen—the pass and the paths to it were utterly deserted, so there was some tincture of mountain solitude here though it was difficult to think of it as an Alpine pass. The col was just below the cloud-base and there was nothing to be seen from it.

Nothing to be seen, that is, in the way of mountains. Of other beautiful things there was abundance. Flowers, the lower-growing alpines, filled the hollows below the pass with drifts of colour and there was alpenrose still blooming on some rock-ledges beside the path. When we stopped for elevenses a little way down (for the pass was crossed before eleven) we perched like mermaids on rocks amid a sea of blue mallow, with globeflower and martagon lily nodding from miniature cliffs above. A shaft of rare sunshine warmed us and lit the mass of blue and yellow colour like a spotlight, against the dark backcloth of pine-clad hillsides lower down.

The path, muddy as ever, curled down through the pines into the Simmental, valley of origin of the famous and beautiful breed of cattle. Well waymarked above, it was unmistakable lower down, for it became an evident local "walk" with rustic seats and picturesque little bridges and was soon a motorable lane with a ski-lift overhead. Lenk, which we were about to enter, is a developing ski-resort and a railway terminal, so we were prepared for its good shops and air of sophistication. While Colin shopped for two luxuries—milk and red wine— I found the *Kurverein* (Tourist Information Office) and settled the undecided question of our onward route from Lenk.

Here at the head of the Simmental we were on the route for the Rawil Pass, which we had tried hard to fit into our west-to-east Oberland traverse for it is the fourth of the quartet of main passes which includes Sanetsch, Gemmi, and Lötschen. We couldn't include it without virtually walking a circle or else missing out the Gemmi, and the alternative plan was to take a high line across the mountains to the Gemmi Pass by way of the Ammertengrat, the Engstligenalp, and the Rote Kumme couloir—an exciting-looking route which Muirhead disparaged with the comment: "Fatiguing; guide 25 fr." At the *Kurverein* they shook grave heads at me. There'd been a lot of new snow high up and the Ammertengrat would be more than merely fatiguing without guide or rope; better to cross to Adelboden and climb to the Engstligenalp, and so to the Gemmi from there. This, then, was the route we followed, but I still think a backpacker could enjoy the Ammertengrat way in a season of fine settled weather.

The six-hour trek over the Trüttlisberg hadn't much fatigued us, a welcome sign that we were becoming used to carrying weights uphill and down; but the climb out of Lenk absorbed every erg we had left. The system we'd now adopted, of contriving to leave a valley in mid-afternoon so as to camp well away from civilisation, is fine for the backpacker when civilisation doesn't climb too high. The new chalets on the mountainside east of Lenk reach a thousand feet above the town and are linked by the lacets of a motorable lane across whose curves the straight *Wanderweg* path, well waymarked, mounts with unyielding steepness. Above this site-less section the path entered slightly wilder terrain of sparse forest and grassy mountainside, but it was all uptilted at a high angle and without one square yard of even approximately level ground. It would soon be dark. A site, and water, had to be found.

> *The world was all before them, where to choose*
> *Their place of rest—*

but Adam and Eve, presumably, were able to find a level spot even outside Paradise.

A torrent could be heard roaring in a precipitous ravine on our left but there was no way of getting at it. We passed a last isolated chalet, decrepit and black with age, perched on a nettle-grown shelf that had no left-over space where a tent might go. The chalet looked deserted, though a thin trickle of water ran in a hollowed-out log beside it. A little way above we dumped our packs and with a cloudy twilight gathering set off in opposite directions to prospect along the slopes. My route took me on a scramble through high-angled pinewoods from which I emerged on the flank of a great knoll overlooking the valley. High up in its side, like a dent in a cathedral dome, I espied a niche whose floor was more or less horizontal, if stony. We lugged the packs up to it, and leaving Colin to pitch the Itisa I took the plastic water-bottle and went back to the ancient chalet, which was at the foot of a steep "ride" between the pines. I collected enough water from the hollow log and was halfway up the steep ride when a grizzled peasant came out of the chalet, stared at me for a moment, and then started up after me with purposeful strides.

The springs of human behaviour are hard to locate. Whether it was because I'd been brought up on John Buchan, or because I'd once for a time tramped Europe with the hands of police and farmers against me, I took to my heels in the opposite direction to that of our camp, doubling back when I was out of sight of the peasant and regaining the tent by a circuitous and singularly painful route.

This idiotic episode didn't spoil the candle-light meal of *rösti*-hash and wine, fruit salad and tea, bread-and-jam and more wine. After it, in the windless dusk outside the tent, we smoked the day's last pipes to the faint music of church bells from the valley and watched the twinkling lights of Lenk a thousand feet below. Away on our left the mass of the Wild-strubel was darkly capped with cloud and night, but the pale glimmer of its glaciers showed under the fringes of the mist. The air was warm and damp and held the certain promise of rain, as I remarked to Colin.

"If it rains," he said brightly, "it'll be for heat."

He was wrong, though. At 9.30 next morning, after we had

toiled for an hour up a steep bare slope much worn by inten-sive skiing, the rain began. Nor did it stop during the rest of that day. On the pass, at 6,410 feet, it was bitterly cold, and when the driving clouds lifted a little from the crags that flanked the glen on the farther side we could see the new snow on their ledges. "The extensive view from here," says Muirhead, "includes the Lohner group and most of the Wildstrubel and Wildhorn range, with the Lauenerhorn and Gifferhorn to the west." If we could have seen it we might have revised our opinion that the Hahnenmoos was the tamest of all our fifteen Oberland passes. It was certainly the most populous by far. There was a small wooden hotel on the pass, reached by a track up which a jeep could drive; and a gang of anoraked children in charge of a teacher; and a party of adults—a club, I think—flying radio-controlled model planes. A sudden strengthening of the rainstorm sent them all scurrying into the hotel as we slogged past in our red Helly Hansen windproofs and on down the zigzag track. The rain was driving as solid as a jet from a hose and as cold as sleet. Five hundred feet below the pass we came to a wooden byre standing on the hillside a few yards from the track and galloped across to it. It was empty, with a nearly waterproof roof and walls whose unshaped logs let in the whistling wind through wide cracks, but it was an opportune shelter from a rainstorm which continued with unabated fury for more than an hour. We got colder and colder.

The classics of the pedestrian journey sing the praises of the roadside fire—let me commend the superior virtues of the propane-gas stove. Our little Bleuet, the S.200 model that weighs 22 ounces with its gas cartridge, purred cheerfully under a billyful of water fetched in a mad rush from a stream a hundred yards away. Vulcan himself couldn't have lit a road-side fire on a day like this, but we got our mugs of hot sweet tea and did a second brew-up as well; the cartridges didn't last long—two-and-a-half days under economical usage—but we could buy another in Adelboden, now four miles and 2,000 feet below us.

A delusive optimism born of tea persuaded us that the rain was less violent and out we plunged into it, splashing at high speed down the broad stony track that was now indistinguishable from a watercourse. Our Helly Hansen windproofs were also proof against rain, but presently the condensation inside them soaked us to the skin. It wasn't an enjoyable descent. Colin's just observation that we might have been freezing on the Ammertengrat instead of sweating in a downpour brought small comfort. When we reached the treeline, however, things looked up. The jeep road here reached a tiny hamlet called Geils, terminus of a motorable road which deposits car-borne tourists at the start of a chairlift by which they can reach the pass without effort. This convenience, it seems, has diverted wayfarers from the old footpath going down by the river, and the path was delightful walking even in the rain. It squeezed through a winding ravine of the forest cheek-by-jowl with the torrent, sometimes crossing it by log bridges that trembled with the vibration of the spate, and the craggy walls above it were hanging-gardens of globeflower and mallow and primula. We looked in vain for a camp-site, and were still looking when the ravine path ejected us suddenly into the sodden cultivation of the wide Engstligental, where camping would involve asking permission from the owner of the ground. Soaked as we were, some chance of drying-out was highly desirable and we were most likely to find it by installing ourselves on the official camp-site at Adelboden. Treading tarmac lanes now, we marched on, downhill into the town.

On such a day, with nothing to be seen of the views, Adelboden was not attractive. It is a sizeable place, long streets of shops and hotels strung across a steep hillside above a deep river-glen, busy with cars and lorries although it stands at the head of the valley with no through road. We located the camp-site, a smallish, poorish place below the town, and found a very muddy place for the tent between the cars and caravans that occupied most of it. Pitching a wet tent in these conditions calls for speed and resolution and we achieved both. The wet rucksacks produced changes of dry clothing—polythene bags, a sovereign tip, were responsible for this miracle—and the tent began to look like home. We left it only to make a sally up to the shops for food, and presently were dining on pilchards in tomato sauce preceded by onion soup and followed by fruit salad. Colin, as always, cooked and served. My part was the washing-up, here a more hygienic operation than usual by reason of an ingenious machine in the site wash-house; you put a twenty-centime piece in a slot and received about a quart of very hot water. By nine it was pitch dark and still raining hard. We nightcapped with tea and biscuits and got into the sleeping-bags, while the rain played a xylophonic lullaby in the puddles outside the tent.

Looking back, it's hard to say whether or not the depressing weather made the three passes between Gsteig and Adelboden the dullest part of the journey. But certainly Adelboden stands out in my recollection as the turning-point, the beginning of true Alpine travel. When, next morning, we turned out in brilliant sunshine and saw the new snow dazzling on the splendid wall of the Wildstrubel over which we were to climb, our hearts lifted up like Wordsworth's when he saw a rainbow in the sky. And Colin, hanging his wet vest on the camp-site fence, hailed the smiling morn with a rendering of *La donn'è mobile* which the close proximity of our neighbours could hardly subdue.

3. ADELBODEN TO LEUKERBAD

Adelboden. Engstligengrat (8,593'). Rote Kumme. Gemmi Pass (7,620'). Leukerbad. 2 days, 2 camps.

One day and one camp should be added here to make up the final total, for we had an off-day at Adelboden. We had been going for a week and it was time we had a Sabbath; moreover, a wire fence on a hot morning is the backpacker's delight for washing-day, and with most of our things already wet it seemed a good idea to finish the job. So we sat about while the "smalls" steamed in the hottest sunlight we'd had yet. But not idly. There were socks to darn and Logs to be written up, while the mud of the camp-site baked hard and the lower slopes of the Wildstrubel above the Engstligen Alp slowly changed from dazzling white to brown and green. It was a further and valid excuse for our loitering that the new snow would have made our passage over to the Gemmi very laborious and possibly a little dicey. All the same, it was disgruntling to sit Achilles-like in one's tent when one had only to lift one's eyes from the darning-needle to see the onward route stretching away for a good six miles to the snowy crests of the main Oberland range.

Adelboden was a turning-point routewise, as well as weatherwise. The north-easterly pass-hopping from Gsteig could have been continued in the same line to bring us to Kandersteg in another twenty-four hours, and thence in another five days or so to Meiringen, all along the northern flank of the Oberland. For anyone with only a fortnight to spare this would be one good route to take; and Colin (who has crossed it) says that the Bonderkrinden Pass, 7,830 feet, between Adelboden and Kandersteg is a notably interesting one. However, our concern on this journey was to see as much of the Bernese Oberland as could be expected by backpackers without rope and axe, and this involved a zigzag or two to cross the Oberland backbone. As the map shows, we were now to head due south from Adelboden, making a hairpin bend from the north-easterly leg; having crossed the Gemmi to the south flank of the Oberland, we would contour the flank until we could recross it by the next break in the line of peaks, the Lötschen Pass, and so arrive at Kandersteg after walking three sides of a rectangle. If a rectangular course can be circuitous, this was. But for splendour and variety of scenery it's the best section of the Oberland Way.

The approach part of the route was laid out, or rather laid up, straight before us as we left the Adelboden camp-site on the morning of Saturday August 5th, the ninth day of our journey. A narrow steep-walled valley ran almost level into the mountains for three miles, to end with dramatic abruptness at the foot of a fifteen-hundred-foot precipice that straddled right across the way and had a long white streak of waterfall down it. Beyond this rim, set back at some distance, were the snows and rock-walls of the Wildstrubel, with the truncated column of the Steghorn to the left of them. Between the Steghorn and the next peak in the rank was the Engstligengrat which we had to cross, but the pass and its eastern summit, the Kindbettihorn, were out of sight behind the precipices of the Lohner closer at hand on our left. In the hidden terrain between the waterfall rim and the Wildstrubel was the Engstligen Alp. Muirhead's *Blue Guide* had revealed that the Alp was accessible by a pathway cut in the side of the precipice ("steep and trying") close to the waterfall, but we had discovered in Adelboden that the enterprising Swiss had lately made it possible to get up by cable-car. Cars were passing us on the narrow lane leading to the Engstligen Fall. It was exceedingly hot. I felt rather glad that instead of camping above the Engstligen Alp, as we had first intended, we were to cross the pass that day—aided by a small piece of cheating.

"You know," Colin had said insinuatingly, "we could catch up on this off-day and have more time in hand. That fifteen hundred feet of path is going to take us three hours, with our packs. But it needn't."

"We use the cable-car?"

"Right. And we'd only need to carry food for one camp because we'd be stocking up in Leukerbad tomorrow."

So glozed the Tempter. And I found it easy enough to swallow my ambition of completing the journey on foot without any benefit of transport; an ambition which, as it happened, I would have been unable to fulfil.

At the valley end, where there is now a car park and a restaurant, we queued with the motor-borne and at last soared upwards in company with twenty-five others. It was a spectacular ride and cost the equivalent of £1 for the two of us. One or two energetic folk could be seen ascending the "steep and trying" path far beneath our suspended globule of glass and metal, and from the sight we hastily averted our eyes. It was just noon when we stepped out of the cable-car.

The Engstligen Alp is one of the most remarkable places in the Swiss Alps. It is an enormous flat-bottomed dish, square in shape, its sides formed by four high mountain ridges each 2½ miles long; the northern corner of the dish is broken off and here the streams of the interior plateau escape down a nearly vertical wall into the green vale south of Adelboden. Its bottom is all lush pasture, with brown specks of cattle grazing in the distance and a few wooden byres. There are also a hotel and a café here, near the terminus of the cable; but these, and a few dozen excursionists wandering near them, were dwarfed and insignificant in the spaciousness of this uplifted prairie and the immensity of the Wildstrubel's north face which glittered across the sky immediately above it. We

2

could see the Kindbettihorn buttresses now, and the snow-sprinkled crest to the right of them where our pass lay. Without bothering to look for waymarks we headed across the flat pastures towards the south-eastern barrier wall of the Alp, rejoicing in the prospect of freedom from tourism and its contrivances and careful not to think of the cable-car.

First on turfy ledges obviously used by venturesome cows we mounted, approaching a steeper glacis of slabs and perched boulders. Red-and-white *Bergweg* waymarks appeared sparsely on the rocks before we had climbed far above the flats and we were soon glad of their marshalling, for the faint and inter-mittent trail disappeared at intervals beneath little snowslopes where our staffs made just the difference between pleasure and anxiety. A snow-slide, even a short one, with a thirty-pound burden on one's back could easily mean an end to that day's travel, at the least. Behind us the endless ridges and glens of the northern Oberland rose into view as we climbed. There was the Hahnenmoos, crossed in pouring rain two days ago, under clear skies now and looking pleasanter, but still tame compared with today's rock and snow. Above on our left the four Dolomite-like spires of a peak euphoniously named the Tschingellochtighorn glowed in the sun. On our right towered a fine rockface topped by a huge overhanging snow cornice. A few more steps on snow, a final scree runnel, and we were on the pass, 8,593 feet.

The Engstligengrat is the name of the ridge we were standing on, and there seems to be no other name for the pass over it—perhaps because it is, in a way, a pass with only one side to it. It overlooks not an immediate descent on the east as might be expected but a wide undulant wilderness of snow and scree; ice too, for into the trough which slopes and steepens down to the north the Ueschinen Glacier pushes its gently-angled tongue. Beyond the trough the snowy terrain spread away lumpily to a rim, an hour or more away, whence the descent to the Gemmi presumably began. Colin and I considered this odd little pass worthy of a name and called it the Kindbetti Pass, for it gave the sudden exciting prospect of new and distant lands which to our way of thinking was the sign-manual of a true pass. As we came up into its rocky nick the first thing we saw was the splendid mass of the Mischabel group thirty miles away in the Valais Alps. These far white summits rose above the rim south-east of the pass. Due east and much nearer were the peaks of Altels and Rinderhorn, with the Balmhorn beyond them. At our feet was beauty in perfect contrast with the giants—masses of alyssum, both white and purple, the flowers giving up their honey-scent to the sunshine.

It was 2.45 and in another two hours we ought to be looking for a camp-site. We lingered only a few minutes on the crest (noting a mountain-rescue kit secured in a niche close to the pass) and then began the slight descent which led to the scree-covered slant of the glacier. A narrow path had been trodden across the one broad streak of snow-covered ice and here again we were glad of our staffs for balance. Looking steeply down to the left on this traverse we saw into the narrow Ueschinental that leads straight down to Kandersteg; in the near foreground a herd of eight bouquetin pottered aimlessly among the boulders. Once we had rounded the head of the glacier trough it was a straightforward business of up-and-down by snow or scree, with one bit of scrambly rock, before we stood on the rim and looked down on the green shores of the Daubensee, in the rift of the Gemmi two thousand feet below. At our feet was a view "which consisted of chasms and crags", with one super-chasm which narrowed as it rose towards us into the semblance of an open-sided well. Down this, as red-and-white waymarks assured us, went the Rote Kumme route. I thought of the ten metres of perlon line we'd bought in Adelboden (in case of encounter with just such a place) and was partly reassured. But the Rote Kumme didn't call for a rope. Very steep indeed it is, but the little path is so neatly engineered that it has no hazards for folk with heads of average steadiness. Its tight zigzags, skipping from the tops of projecting rocks into narrow corners and out and down again, took us steadily down a thousand feet to easier ground. Another five hundred feet and we were out of cold shadow into evening sunshine and a miniature rock-garden. Vast cliffs, smooth and pink-tinted, rose on either hand to frame the saffron snows of the Rinder-horn in front, but at their feet were grassy dells where sheep grazed, tinkling their bells beside a singing stream that danced down from one paradisal camping place to another. We pitched at six o'clock, on a level sward of grass and gentians beside the stream where the morning sun would strike the tent as soon as it cleared the Rinderhorn shoulder opposite. Rugged arms of silver-grey rock embraced the site, with pink androsacae and dryas octopetala growing in their niches. It was a dream of a place—a good lightweight-camper's dream—and our meal that evening was of a quality and quantity to match. With Leukerbad only a few hours away down the Gemmi we could afford to be lavish.

Even the washing-up was a joy in such a place. You strolled across the carpet of gentians (the flowers closing now in the twilight) to the rock-basin fed by a little waterfall; and returned with the clean mugs and plates, stumbling a bit because the sunset-glow on the high snows made it impossible to keep your eyes on your feet. We needed no lullaby that night. But if we had done, there was the quiet song of the stream and the sleepy tinkle of the sheep-bells.

And so, next morning, to the Gemmi, possibly the most remarkable of Alpine passes and certainly one of the oldest. Again it was a day of hot sun. The Rote Kumme path debouched from its tilted canyon two or three hundred feet below where we had camped and turned due south above the west shores of the mud-coloured Daubensee, paralleling a rank of tall pylons carrying power-lines. How easily we have come to accept these things as a normal incident in mountain scenery! I felt only a transient irritation at having to march alongside their iron feet, round which—by some unfathomable charity of Nature—the carpet of Alpine flowers was denser and more brilliant than anywhere else on the lake shore. In any case, the pylons were only a gentle introduction to worse ugliness on the crest of the pass. Our path rounded the end of the lake, joined the much broader main track from Kandersteg, and arrived in a few more minutes at a clutter of graceless buildings on the brink of the famous limestone precipice. Concrete and wood and iron had been heaped into incongruous shapes housing hotel, toilets and the top station of the cable-cars that came dangling up from Leukerbad. Mark Twain, tramping to this point a century ago, wrote afterwards: "We were surrounded by a hideous desolation. We stepped forward, and were confronted by a startling contrast; we seemed to look down into fairyland." The desolation of his day was the rather unprepossessing wilderness that undulates at this end of the Daubensee between the crags of Plattenhorner and Daubenhorn, but the Swiss, usually more careful in such matters, have since made it worse. Averting our eyes, we too stepped forward. The aerial view of Leukerbad's concrete hotels, shrunk to pebble size amid toy hills very far below, didn't suggest fairyland to us. More enchanting by far was the array of ivory peaks that floated on the haze above and beyond the invisible Rhone valley. Dom and Täschhorn were there, the Arolla peaks, Matterhorn and Dent Blanche and lesser summits unidentifiable, transformed from the solid chunks of Earth on which we had kicked and clung our way in years gone by into the insubstantial battlements of Heaven. It was nice to think that they'd still be looking like that when the last block of concrete had crumbled into dust.

The cliff that falls from this viewpoint is the lowest part of the great limestone wall that supports the Oberland glaciers and snows on the south side. Whether you look from its top or up at it from Leukerbad, its verticalities appear quite impassable except by some modern hardman equipped with all the paraphernalia of artificial climbing; in fact, the extraordinary path that creeps a lizardly way up their 3,000 feet has been used by travellers for centuries and latterly by several generations of tourists. Mark Twain descending this path in 1878 met "an everlasting procession of guides, porters, mules, litters, and tourists climbing up". When Colin and I began a cautious descent we met only tourists, and by no means an everlasting procession; possibly the current spread of tourism has also spread the tourists, deconcentrating them from the dozen indispensable spectacles of the Swiss Tour of which the Gemmi Pass was one. Despite the intense heat (we were in shorts and shirts) most of the ascending folk wore thick breeches and stockings and heavy wool sweaters, the exception being a pretty girl in a bikini swimsuit and pumps. The girl looked a great deal happier than the others.

The rock-wall of the Gemmi faces south-south-east. We were able to note on this day and the next morning that it is in full sunshine from 7 a.m. to 4 p.m. in August; a fact worth remembering by anyone walking the Oberland Way from east to west. A backpacker, for instance, would be well advised to start up the path after the sun has left it and make that night's camp by the Daubensee, unless he can face a start at five in the morning. Much better, though, to descend, as we did, if only for the stirring views. Cunning zigzags took us down the face of a buttress and then round on to the sheer wall of a couloir. Sometimes there was an overhang below us, sometimes an overhang above, and in places the way was a rectangular groove incised in a vertical cliff, with always the same steep downward angle. Halfway down, having passed the last of the ascending tourists, we halted on a corner that was like the capital of a giant Corinthian column to spy out the land below us and trace our onward route from Leukerbad.

The steep and forested shoulder of the Torrenthorn had risen to hide the Valais mountains now. From the little town at its foot road, river and railway (a narrow-gauge electric line) followed the glen rightward to a corner below which, but unseen, was the Rhone Valley. We could see an oblong of glaring unnatural blue just below the town—a swimming-pool; Leukerbad is of course a spa, with hot saline springs and bath-houses which were built as long ago as 1501. But in this depot of tourism we proposed to linger only as long as it took us to buy food for the next section of the journey, which would take us up and round the Torrenthorn shoulder, across an 8,000-foot pass to the flank of the Lötschental, and over the glacier-pass to the Gasterntal and Kandersteg, a route that kept high above villages or other supply-points. It was a little after noon. We would make two or three hours' going beyond Leukerbad and camp on the hither side of the first pass, the Resti. But the best-concerted schemes, as we were soon to learn, die fast away.

The last zigzag of the path straightened and broadened into a dusty mule-track down a scree of limestone boulders. The foot-slopes of the Gemmi are entirely waterless—it would be a poor place to camp—and we ate a late and dry lunch in the shade of the first tree we came to. Leukerbad, when we entered its narrow streets, provided water from a wooden trough in its more ancient part, a small nucleus of wooden chalets embedded in new villas and blocks of flats. In the hot afternoon its streets were still and Sunday-like—and, indeed, it *was* Sunday.

When I was a boy there was much talk of the sinful

"Continental Sunday" whereon all the gay Europeans made merry (and money) instead of going to church like the respectable British. Half-a-century later Britain had gone at least part of the way into Europe and there was no need for a wayfarer to go short of food or entertainment in England on the Sabbath. But here in Leukerbad, in the very heart of the non-Godfearing Continong, we were back with the English Sunday. Every shop, store, office and bar was firmly and irrevocably shut until tomorrow.

"It's a judgment," I said, "for using that cable-car. If we hadn't, we'd have got here on Monday."

"We can't cross two high passes on a packet soup and two inches of loaf," said Colin. "Let's get on up the trail for an hour and pitch the tent. Early tomorrow morning we slip down here without the packs and stock up."

There was really nothing else to be done. The broad pathway to the Torrent Alp began at the south end of the upper village and for an hour or more we toiled slowly up it in broiling afternoon sunshine until at last, a little way along a level track on the left, a site for the tent was found. It was a small shelf of deep grass under pines above a bank where bilberries grew, and on the hillside above the pines a stocky brown-faced man was breaking the Leukerbadian Sabbath by repairing a fence. Since this was probably his land, I clambered up to him and asked if we might camp there.

"Camp where you like—where you like," he told me in very fair English, and waved away my hint of payment.

It wasn't an ideal camp-site but it had a view right across the Leukerbad valley to the Daubenhorn and the Gemmi. When I'd fetched water (in the quite invaluable polythene bucket) from a stream a quarter-mile back down the path and we'd quenched an inordinate thirst with several pints of tea the place began to feel like home, as a camp-site should. Supper of heel-of-a-loaf and soup left us with half-a-dozen biscuits for breakfast tomorrow. We watched the twilight rise like a dark tide to fill the glen below and tiny yellow stars twinkle out from the windows of the hotel on the pass. The cliffs of the Gemmi looked like Cyclopean lock-gates stemming the tide, grey and sheer and surely quite unclimbable.

4. LEUKERBAD TO KANDERSTEG

Leukerbad. Resti Pass (8,658'). Kummenalp chalets. Lötschen Pass (8,825'). Kandersteg. 3 days, 2 camps.

Perhaps to compensate for Sunday Closing, the Leukerbad shops opened at 8 on Monday morning. Colin and I were ready and waiting with our plastic shopping-bag, an article almost as essential to Continental backpacking as a folding polythene bucket. Carrying food for three days—no great burden, on our exiguous diet—we sped back up the forest path to where we had left the packs hidden in a thicket. At just after 9 on this eleventh day of the journey we were on our way.

Red-and-white waymarks guided us up a smaller and steeper path climbing the wooded flank of the Torrenthorn, soon traversing at the foot of a wall of cliff. It was a hot morning, but here we were in cool shade with a multitude of woodland flowers nodding from the boulders above and below. This idyllic progress lasted for a brief hour and then was exchanged for a long and very steep slog up a turfy nose in full sunlight; an ascent made even less attractive by the raw new scars and buildings of a cableway under construction. By now it is no doubt in operation, connecting some point in the valley with the hut or hotel we could see perched below the red crags of the Torrenthorn overhead. With relief we bore away to the right, across the head of a grassy couloir below the hotel, and in a few minutes were round a rocky corner and out of sight of man's untidy contrivings.

The route-finding hereabouts required the use of map and compass and a modicum of common sense, for the *Bergweg* marks had disappeared and I don't recall seeing them again during the rest of this day. However, the weather was clear and the path we were now on was at the right height and leading in the right direction, north-east by east. It was little more than a sheep-track contouring easily below the shattered Torrenthorn cliffs on the left, with deep bare cwms down on the right where the brown dots of cattle moved slowly. Beyond the cwms, and very far below, the silver ribbon of the Rhone lay coiled on the green velvet of its valley, with the snows of the Pennine Alps shining like a long curtain of white silk stretched behind and above. When we took a five-minute halt and looked behind us to the south-west, there was Mont Blanc, a pinkish wraith of a mountain, hanging in the mid-air haze sixty miles away. The mountainside was wild and free and beautiful with flowers, the delightful path was utterly deserted (in the first week of August!) as we had grown to expect these paths to be; it was impossible not to think of the processions that would be encountered on mountain paths in North Wales and the Lake District on a day like this. We did in fact see five people, the only ones, as we descended from the minor col towards the small lake called the Weisssee—a family party lunching and paddling. It was no mean achievement, I thought, to get small children to a spot as high and solitary as this.

The Weisssee lies in a vast stony hollow and the Resti Pass stands above it. Seen from the west side, it is a model of what a pass should be. Two bold 9,000-foot rock peaks, Resti Rothorn on the north and Laucherspitze on the south, overlook the wide and deep V of the pass. Rock ribs flecked with snow mount to the notch of the V, which shows nothing but empty sky beyond it—to my mind an important attribute of the ideal pass, on which the achievement of looking from it into hitherto unseen country is the equivalent of gaining a mountain summit. We gloated over this beautiful pass as we lunched in the partial shade of a boulder near the Weisssee. It was a dry lunch, for the little lake is only a couple of inches deep and has a mud bottom; there were no streams hereabouts and we didn't regret the delay that had prevented us from camping on this side of the Resti. The faint track up to the pass, long and steep with the sun beating on our backs, provided us with the much-needed drink a little before we reached the crest, where a melting snow-patch somewhere above sent down an ice-cold trickle. The sort of physical fitness that comes after ten days' backpacking had sent us along like bombs all day, and with this revivifying draught inside us we fairly galloped up the final snow mounds to the rocks of the pass. And halted—spellbound, as they say.

At our feet the full-length magnificence of the Lötschental stretched away to the far white saddle of the Lötschenlucke, a green avenue flanked by a double row of snow-peaks. The glaciers shone like emeralds in their rock settings above the walls of forest and the Bietschhorn shrugged an enormous

2*

shoulder close above on the right. But—for me more lovely than these—two distant white summits nodded from beyond the Lötschenlucke: Finsteraarhorn and Aletschhorn, old friends, greeted now after an absence of twenty-five years. Perhaps I may be forgiven the emotional gulp that held me silent while Colin was striding up and down in exclamatory ecstasies.

"Aren't you *impressed*, man?" he demanded with true South Walian fervour.

I hastened to assure him that I was. Indeed! On which he calmed down somewhat and we took a snack, with all that mountain splendour spread before us. We had passed clumps of glacier crowfoot on the way up, and now, here at 8,658 feet, there were scented cushions of white alyssum. From Leukerbad to the pass had taken us seven hours, and as an eight-hour day is quite enough for even well-broken-in backpackers it was resolved to find a camp-site a thousand feet down on the other side; if we could.

We could and did. Unlike the west side of the Resti, the east side is green and well watered. As soon as the path (pleasant and easy though steep) had brought us down some craggy scree we began to spot desirable tent emplacements in flowery nooks, each with water laid on in the shape of sparkling rivulets. The angle of descent eased, for our way now was along the flank of the Schwarzhorn with the Lötschental below on the right, and in another mile or so we would be turning sharply uphill to the left (north) to cross the main range again. A big ravine opened on the right, dropping to the valley, and on the lip of this a hundred feet below the path was a grassy ledge or promontory across which a little stream dawdled before taking the plunge into the chasm. The place was somewhat exposed to the gusty wind blowing down from the peaks overhead but we pitched here, securing the tentpegs with rocks, and occupied the most romantically-sited camp of the journey, at 7,500 feet. This, as I remarked to Colin, is what mountain backpacking is about. There's little point in humping a tent over 8,000-foot passes if you're going to camp in a place you could have driven a car to.

We slept sound and warm on our eyrie and woke to find the Lötschental brimming with white mist that overflowed the tent. The mist moved upwards and began to break as we broke our fast, the Bietschhorn was clearing while the tent was being folded and packed, and by the time we were swinging down the path the wayside gentians were wide-eyed to a clear blue sky. Belled cattle in charge of a herd-boy clanked and jangled up the path from the Resti chalets clustered on a sunlit promontory below. Past these chalets the Lötschen Pass route mounted from Ferden in the valley 2,000 feet below, two miles from Goppenstein where the main railway line to Kandersteg enters the Lötschberg Tunnel; to this route we had perforce to descend in order to turn the precipices at the end of the Schwarzhorn ridge, joining it where it ascended to the herdsmen's chalets on the Kummenalp. Colin, who had crossed the Pass two years earlier, remembered Kummenalp as ancient and remote, a tiny community content to exist here at nearly 7,000 feet with only a thread of steep track to connect it with the valley. It was no longer so. The track up to Resti had been made motorable and an extension was being excavated up the one-in-three mountainside to Kummenalp. Already a bold motorist might force his car right up to the herdsmen's chalets, and the inevitable had followed: more than half the dozen or so picturesque wooden dwellings had been converted into holiday homes, with incongruous modern extensions and new roofs suggestive of Suburbia. There was a little *gasthof* where we drank small glasses of milk at large prices and chatted with two German girls who were apparently proposing to wander over the glaciers in plimsolls. Then we shook the cement dust of Kummenalp from our feet and began a very steep 2,000-foot climb.

The Lötschen is a mountain-walker's pass. Among the more energetic of the Kandersteg habitués its crossing confers a certain distinction. It is a glacier pass, it is not far short of 9,000 feet, and if you cross it from north to south you have 3,500 feet of very steep ascent and 4,500 feet of steep descent to do. A popular expedition is the crossing from Kandersteg to Goppenstein and return by rail through the Lötschberg Tunnel, and as we toiled upwards in very hot sunshine we met seven or eight small parties descending on this round. None of them were British. This was our twelfth day and we had not en-countered a single English person; though we had heard an American in Gsteig.

Kummenalp had been left at 10.20; at 12.10 we halted for lunch in a nook of flowers where ice-cold water trickled down a slab, and at 12.50 were standing beside the big wooden cross on the top of the pass. The upper section of the path was very steep and slithery, though by no means perilous, and emerged on a broad saddle of rock and snow under the tremendous precipices of the Balmhorn, with blue snow-lakes dotted here and there and the Grosse Doldenhorn stabbing into the blue sky beyond the unseen depths of the Gasterntal. Possibly because we'd exhausted our raptures on the less famous Resti Pass the very fine views were soberly appreciated rather than exclaimed about. Moreover, our arrival on the Resti had had the advantage of complete solitude and freedom from any sign of tourism; here there was a spruce wooden hut complete with Swiss flag (refreshments but no accommodation) and half-a-dozen people resting and lunching. It's a form of snobbishness, perhaps, to wish to have a lofty and beautiful place to oneself, but if it is then I'm a snob in company with Wordsworth, Milton, Byron and a great many others.

There was a good deal more snow lying on the north side of the Lötschen Pass. The descent began by crossing one or two small snowfields between emergent slabs where cairns were perched. Cairns and waymarks made the whole of this day's route easy to follow, and only in a dense mist or a snowstorm could a normally observant walker miss the way. Colin, I think, had wanted to go down the glacier itself, which was easy-angled snow with no crevasses to speak of, but I had already gone ahead on the line of the *Bergweg* marks, which bore away to the right along the fringe of rock and moraine and discharged us in a brief glissade on to the glacier a little above its snout. It was a broad and dirty snout of mingled ice and scree a couple of hundred yards across, ending in a rubble of boulders on the lip of a sheer drop. We trod the slanting surface with exaggerated caution, having watched two nervous tourists making heavy weather of the crossing; but it was perfectly safe and easy, and leaving the sweating pair to recover on a boulder we swung on down a path of innumerable zigzags. From the glacier lip we had been able to look into the head of the Gasterntal down on the right, where the Kander glacier spills over a cliff from the wide snow-basin rimmed by

Blümlisalphorn, Gspaltenhorn and Tschingelhorn. Now we were descending into the trough-like valley at the point where it makes a right-angled bend north-westward towards Kandersteg. By four o'clock we were down at the treeline and drinking milk at the delightfully-placed little inn on the Gfällalp, milk that was considerably more expensive than the red wine we were accustomed to drink in camp. Nothing, as Shakespeare pointed out, "confounds a man so much as a great reckoning in a little room"; but the charms of the continuing downward path, beside a spectacular waterfall and through steep woodlands where dark-brown squirrels leapt overhead, quickly comforted us. A wooden bridge crossed to the right bank of the roaring glacier-torrent in the valley bottom and we turned left on the motorable lane down the Gasterntal.

A million postcards and a century of travellers' eulogies have broadcast the wonders of the Gasterntal and it's still a stupendous place, three-and-a-half miles of narrow green levels between soaring rock-walls with hardly a break in their continuous verticality. Walking down it, you need a rubber neck. Every few minutes a new waterfall appears spouting from some nick in the skyline directly overhead, dispatched from the glaciers of the Doldenhorn on the north or the Balmhorn on the south. With this marvel of Nature the Swiss have done better than they have with the Gemmi Pass. The lane is closed to motoring tourists and a minibus runs two or three times a day to the hamlet of Selden in the upper valley. Such artificial seclusion, much the lesser of two evils, inevitably carries with it an unwelcome touch of "preservation", and Colin (who had been here before) had an idea that camping in the Gasterntal was frowned upon by authority. However, we had been going for nearly nine hours, no camp-site had offered itself on the Gfällalp, and we were tired. In a charming grassy glade between trees on the left of the lane we chanced it.

With so much water tumbling from the skies and rushing along a stone's-throw away it was odd that there was nothing to drink. The glacier stream was grey with mud and grit and the waterfalls mysteriously vanished before they reached the valley. I had to fetch water from a spring twenty minutes farther on along the lane before we could dine—chicken soup, hard-boiled eggs, and nectarous camel-draughts of tea—at seven o'clock. Twilight brimmed in the Gasterntal, loud with the voices of falling water. Two vehicles, local farm trucks, had passed me as I went and returned on my water-fetching but now the valley was utterly deserted. We had a visitor, though; more accurately, perhaps, a hostess. A solitary and beautiful Simmental cow inhabited the glade and took a very close interest in our dinner menu, her large bell clanging loudly every time she ducked her head to look into the tent. Cows may ordinarily be termed "beautiful" only in comparison with other cows, but I think the Swiss variety compare favourably, as to looks, with some human beings. Smoking a final pipe, I considered our Simmental lady beside a memory of some stout and energetic German ladies we had encountered on the other side of the Lötschen Pass. Doubtless the latter were good wives and *hausfraus*, but I knew which I preferred to look at.

At eight the candle was lit in our tent. At nine the circumambulant bell-ringing became intermittent and ceased. We and our lady-friend slept.

One of the most striking things about the Gasterntal (we discovered when we walked on down it next morning) is the way in which its western exit appears to be completely barred by a wall of cliffs. You would swear that the Kander river that foams along beside you must of necessity go underground to reach Kandersteg. But at the last moment, so to speak, lane and river double sharply to the right through a remarkable rift barely wide enough for the two of them, and a last half-mile of descent—passing through two tunnels in the rock—brings you down to the main road and the sophistications of the valley. It's another two miles of road and paved sidewalks into Kandersteg and for Colin and me they were very hot miles. At a clothing shop on the outskirts of the town I bought a pair of shorts to replace the ones I had on, which had nothing to recommend them except ample ventilation; in a centre so devoted to culture (Yehudi Menuhin has an annual summer concert here and the local theatre was advertising a Chekhov play) and where we might actually meet a British visitor, it was up to me to look respectable, at any rate from the waist down.

Kandersteg is a pleasant place. Even in the dusty heat of an

August noon, even with the parading tourists and the souvenir shops and the cars processing towards the station to be shipped through the Lötschberg Tunnel, it retained its charm. "Whichever way you look, you see mountains or glaciers," says the tourist brochure; and it is so. We had planned from the first to spend a day here looking round, which meant two nights on the official camp-site, so we made at once for the Rendezvous, a big site set well back from the main road at the foot of the Oeschinensee chairlift. There are two official camp-sites at Kandersteg and we had passed the other just after leaving the foot of the Gasterntal; it looked a quieter and less sophisticated place than Rendezvous but was more than a mile from the shops, bank, and information office, all of which we needed to visit.

The Rendezvous was fairly crowded with caravans and dormobiles. The best place we could find for the tent was a corner almost directly below the ascending cables of the *Sesselbahn*. But the site had everything—showers, hot water, washing-up place, and even a pair of British tourists, the only ones we'd encountered. With the middle-aged couple from Sheffield in a home-conversion dormobile we exchanged experiences, and then sauntered into town to buy tomatoes and apricots, the latter a good buy at this time of year.

Lunching outside the tent, we were a perfect bomb-target for any ill-disposed persons who happened to occupy the two-seater "chairs" which passed continuously overhead. All that came down to us, however, was an occasional *"Bon appetit!"* as a French holiday-maker in transit spotted us, and we finished the apricots unscathed.

5. KANDERSTEG TO LAUTERBRUNNEN

Kandersteg. Hohtürli Pass (8,880'). Steinenberg. Sefinen Furgge (8,583'). Mürren. Lauterbrunnen. 3½ days, 3 camps.

"Whichever way you look, you see mountains or glaciers." And that was just my trouble. *Dolce far niente* was a philosophy for rainy days; the onward route led straight up from our tent to the rock and snow of the next pass—the very chairlifters were spidering up that way every half-minute or so—and the morning of our proposed off-day was clear and sunny. In Kandersteg they said that the whole of July had been bad weather in the Alps and the present fine spell wouldn't last much longer. Having woken Colin with a cuppa calculated to render him amenable, I proposed that we should use the morning of the "off-day" in stocking up and the afternoon in getting into position for the crossing of our twelfth and highest pass, the Hohtürli. "But I've only had ten hours' sleep," he objected. This, however, was no more than a token protest and we prepared to leave the Rendezvous in the early afternoon.

Most of the "smalls" had been washed and dried on the afternoon of our arrival, and we had changed travellers' cheques and visited the Tourist Information Bureau, as always a productive visit. The director of the *Verkehrsverein* had been helpful. We learned from him (without divulging our own sleeping-place of two nights ago) that the authorities did not countenance camping in the lower Gasterntal. We also learned that the Hohtürli Pass was free from snow and that the steep descent on its east side was protected with a fixed wire rope. On hearing that we were bound for the Hohtürli, moreover, he presented us—disregarding our halfhearted protests—with free passes on the chairlift to the Oeschinensee path; to neglect to take advantage of this generosity, we agreed, would be both churlish and uneconomical. So at 1.30 of a very hot afternoon we and our packs whirred and clanked upward from pylon to pylon to be discharged on a broad path at about 5,000 feet, a path dotted with strolling tourists and leading in an easy mile to the Oeschinensee.

Practically every travel agency in Britain has on display a picture of the blue Oeschinensee with the snow-peaks and glaciers of the Blümlisalphorn above. It's just like that. There were a few boats on the lake and plenty of people about, but for once I was able to feel pleased that so many non-mountaineers were able—thanks to the Swiss genius for such things— to set eyes on so lovely a sight. Maybe our own use of the chairlift was responsible for this benevolent attitude, for I was even more pleased to discover that few non-mountaineers (or, at least, few strolling tourists) were likely to get far along the Hohtürli path once it had turned to the left off the main track

Above the Lizerne cleft. La Fava (8,568) feet behind

The Swiss "Grade 2" official campsite at Gsteig

Path to the Kindbetti Pass over the Engstligengrat (8,593 feet)

Approaching the Resti Pass (8,658 feet) from the west

The tent above the Lötschental, at 7,500 feet

Looking back up the Lötschen Glacier towards the pass

Path to the Hohtürli. The pass (8,880 feet) is seen below and left of the Blümlisalp Hut on the skyline

just short of the lake shore. It mounted unfenced round the impressive buttresses overlooking the eastern end of the Oeschinensee, struck up steep rocky mountainside, and climbed some little vertical crags where fixed ropes assisted balance. Above these we came to the small Ober Bergli chalet on the lip of a wild upper basin of pasture in the lap of splendid mountains. The chalet, inhabited in summer from about the end of June onwards, has sleeping accommodation under the rafters at three francs a night and you can buy soup and bread. We had glasses of milk, and noted once again that it was no better than the milk to be bought at one-third the price in the Co-op of any Swiss tourist centre.

It was nearing five o'clock. We tramped on up the path with an eye open for a likely camp-site. In front the glen narrowed and rose steeply towards the sérацs of the Blümlisalp glacier, on which sat the stumpy rock-peak of the Stock with the snow-ridges of Weisse Frau and Morgenhorn above and beyond. Half-a-mile short of the glacier we offed packs and spent twenty minutes looking for a flat space among the piles of huge silver-grey boulders below the path; time well spent, for when we found a site it was the choicest camping-place of all. A glacier torrent rumbled nearby for washing in, there was clear drinking water five minutes away, white dryas and helianthemum decorated the niches of the boulders and deep-pink alpenrose filled the spaces between them. We were at 6,500 feet here, with high peaks so close above us that the sun was off our tent before 6.30. At just after 9, when I went outside, the torrent had shrunk to a rivulet and its bass rumble was now a gentle murmur. The peaks stood ghostly against a sky of brilliant stars, and a meteor flashed across above the glimmering white bulk of the Doldenhorn.

But it was a mistake to camp a mere fifteen minutes from the Ober Bergli chalet. As we sipped our expensive milk there we had made a vain attempt to chat with a pair of juvenile cowherds attached to the place, and when—as we sat smoking in the tent by candlelight—we heard smothered laughter among the boulders outside we didn't doubt that these youngsters were prowling round in the starlight. Nothing untoward in this, perhaps; but next morning our faithful staffs, which we'd left leaning against a rock a few yards away, were missing, and this was less tolerable. Not only had we become much attached to these sticks in the fourteen days since we cut them in the thickets of Fontannaz-Seulaz, but we had also come to rely on them for safe balancing on precipitous paths. We marched down to the Ober Bergli full of righteous wrath to demand restitution. But now behold a miracle. The folk at the chalet, who yesterday could speak some English and more French, were today unable to comprehend a word of either language; and there was no sight or sound of any youngsters. We gave up, went back to breakfast in warm sunshine, and were away staffless by nine o'clock.

From this point onwards the path climbs very steeply into mountain scenery of increasing grandeur, emerging from an uptilted maze of gullies and bluffs to follow the crest of a giant moraine piled against the cliffs on the north side of a ravine a thousand feet deep. Across the ravine you look straight into the green crevasses on the icefall of the Blümlisalp glacier—if, that is, you can raise your eyes from the essential business of watching your step. For this magnificent path clings to slopes on which a fall would mean broken limbs at the least; and in its upper section the topheavy backpacker cannot afford the least slip of the foot. As well as being a pass route the path is the way to the large Blümlisalp Hut of the Swiss Alpine Club and receives heavy usage. This "human erosion" had scraped away the scree of the last steep bit and laid bare a glacis of rock so smooth that vibram soles could scarcely get footing on it, and since the glacis overhung a snow couloir that swept down to the lip of the ravine I teetered very gingerly up it, wishing heartily for the extra steadying my missing staff would have afforded. I found this brief final section a trifle scaring, I must admit; but the difficulty of balancing the two-stone pack was solely responsible for the uncertainty, and I must emphasise that the whole route over the Hohtürli has no difficulty and little real danger for an average mountain-walker in good trim. Colin, who had been on the stony saddle of the pass for ten minutes when I got there, restored my diminished ego by declaring that the glacis was the diciest bit of the whole journey.

On the Hohtürli Pass, 8,880 feet, the distant views are restricted and dwarfed by the magnificence of the immediate surroundings. Huge crags, snow-walls and bergschrunds, the impending white cone of the Wilde Frau and the triple glacier of the Blümlisalp—all are strikingly close at hand. The S.A.C. hut stands a few hundred feet above the saddle to destroy the humble walker's illusion that he has somehow got into a sanctuary of the high Alps attainable only by experienced climbers. We were on this pass at 11 a.m., having despite our burdens climbed 4,000 feet in two hours, for we were now at the very peak of fitness. This had induced in me another illusion: that physical efficiency was the real yardstick when it came to measuring age, and that the passing of Time could be ignored. A massive young German who had followed me up the last half-mile of the path was the destroyer of this one. As we stood on the pass he accosted me in excellent English.

"Your pardon, sir, but you are a wonderful walker," said he. "May I ask your age?"

All the vanished decades came back like homing pigeons as I told him.

Besides the young German, we met a party of half-a-dozen German senior scouts on the Hohtürli. Coached by a competent leader, they set off down the eastern side on the route we were to follow, and we watched their slitherings and contortions in some anxiety. On this side crags and snowslopes fell away very steeply into a great bare couloir. The route traversed leftward above these into a gully, scarcely less steep, which occupied the angle between the slopes and some overhanging cliffs. You could fall for some hundreds of feet down this gully, but the possibility was partly obviated by a very long wire rope that dangled down it, pegged into the wall of cliff in places but with its bottom end lying loose. I welcomed Colin's suggestion (made, I think, for my benefit) that we should use our 10-metre perlon line for safeguarding here, and we tied on. But in fact the difficulty was less than it appeared, and in ten minutes the potential danger of a slip and a long fall was gone. We unroped and scuttled down scree for an hour, rounding a corner out of the bare couloir into a broader glen descending parallel to it on the west, where easier terrain and a stream with gentians growing near it invited a halt for lunch at 1.15. The wooded Kiental was directly below us now and the after-lunch route dropped into it down a ridge of stones and turf that was furrowed as if some mad ploughman and his team had tried to cultivate it, but the path was plain all the way down to the chalets of Oberbund, a small and primitive place. There is a bunkhouse and a sort of restaurant here, so one could make a non-camping crossing of the Hohtürli by sleeping at Ober Bergli—first hiding one's staff—and using Oberbund for the next night's lodging. We, of course, were for a camp-site; and when the last thousand feet of that 4,000-foot descent had brought us into the upper glen of the Kiental, Colin found a delightful site on a rock-bluff crowned with pines.

We pitched the tent and had a brew-up; one of those memorable brew-ups with forest-scents and waterfall-music to emphasise the comfortable fact that the heat and toil of the day are over; when a magnum of Mouton Rothschild would be as ditchwater compared with three mugs of sweet milkless tea. After it we strolled down a riverside track to Steinenberg, a charming hamlet at the head of the Kiental twenty minutes below our camp. It had very recently been made possible for cars to reach Steinenberg and sometimes, it seemed, they paid dearly for the privilege. Three weeks earlier there had been a vast landslide, following the torrential rains of July, which had buried three chalets and two cars and formed a new lake just below the village. More motorists than ever, they told us, were now driving up from Thun and Spiez to see the new lake.

In the little Steinenberg store there was a bottle of wine labelled *TOSCA*. This twofold appeal to Colin's tastes was not to be resisted. That night we celebrated our feats of the day with Tosca and cigars; and thereafter dropped into sound sleep like stones dropping into a deep, still pool.

Next day we crossed the Sefinen Furgge; a day of sorrow and not to be lingered on, since in the early part of it I lost my pipe.

The main track up the valley ran through the woods not far above our camping-place, and half-a-mile up it, just after crossing a wooden bridge over a side-stream, a well-marked path struck up to the left into the mouth of a steep glen. Zigzagging round cliff corners and climbing rock bluffs crowned with grass and flowers, it conducted us into a wild upper ravine which an earlier generation would justly have called "savage". The day was one of hazy sunshine and oppressively hot. We took the ascent easily, stopping for a ten-minute smoke after an hour's going at a spot whence (I believe) there were splendid backward views of the Hohtürli and the Blümlisalp range but which is dulled and blackened in memory because it was here that I left my pipe.

Memory blurs the last hour of the ascent, too, but this is because the Sefinen Furgge from the west is not at all unlike the Hohtürli. The surroundings are less snowy and there is no spectacular glacier just across the way, but there is the same narrow path across uncomfortable scree-slopes and the same ticklish scramble ("They need a fixed rope here," panted Colin) up bare slabs near the top. The pass itself, a narrow saddle between crags, is more dramatic than the Hohtürli. The rock crest is only a yard or two wide, and as you poke your head above it there they are—the famous three, Eiger and Mönch and Jungfrau, superbly poised above the Lauterbrunnen precipices.

We lunched here—it was 12.45—sitting on the sunwarmed base of a crag from which two singularly tame choughs flew down at intervals for the crumbs. It was a place to pause and savour time and distance, the fifteen days that stretched away behind us to Bex and the week of travel that was left; for the Sefinen Furgge was the last of the worthy passes between Bex and Meiringen. Kleine Scheidegg and Grosse Scheidegg were still to cross, both topping 6,000 feet and famous for their scenery, but these would be very different from this lofty notch where we and the choughs had the Alpine world to ourselves. Or did have. Voices drifting up from the invisible eastern slopes below apprised us of coming invasion, and we shouldered packs and started down, passing a party of middle-aged Germans who had come up from Mürren.

This descent was very easy compared with the way we had come up. Twenty minutes of zigzagging down scree, and we were striding down a good path across the lower slopes of the Hundshorn. And striding fast. A glance backward had shown us a huge black cloud spreading out above the pass like a foul bombard that would shed his liquor, and with us as with Trinculo here was neither bush nor shrub to bear off any weather at all—nor a practicable camp-site. It was nearly three o'clock and we were a thousand feet down when the pass disappeared behind a veil of rain. We dashed for a flattish place a hundred yards from the path, pitched the tent in record time, and scrambled inside with our gear just as the storm broke.

Huckleberry Finn was a better hand at describing a thunderstorm than Byron or Wordsworth: "*Fst!* it was as bright as glory; dark as sin again in a second, and now you'd hear the thunder let go with an awful crash and then go rumbling, grumbling, tumbling down the sky towards the under side of the world, like rolling empty barrels downstairs, where it's long stairs and they bounce a good deal, you know." In that mountain-enclosed hollow the noise was deafening. Wind and lashing rain roared in the intervals between the thunder-crashes and conversation was next to impossible. Inside the tent we were dry and snug in spite of having no flysheet. The first hosepipe-like impact of the rain had driven a very fine spray through the fabric for two or three seconds and then the weave had tightened and sealed; nor did it let in one drop more during the $2\frac{1}{2}$ hours of exceedingly heavy rain. The Itisa weighed just under 10 lbs—fairly heavy for a lightweight tent—and I'd decided not to add the $3\frac{3}{4}$-lb flysheet, an extra which besides doubling the time taken to erect the tent means certain trouble in high winds. This severe test fully justified the decision. The heavy sewn-in groundsheet, slightly "dished" at the edges, also justified itself. Halfway through the phenomenal rainstorm the floor on which we lay creased into ridges and furrows as the surface water racing down the mountainside behind us flowed beneath it, but we stayed high and dry as on a raft anchored in a tideway.

At six the thunderstorm was over, though the rain continued steadily for another hour. I made a sally to get water—there were foaming cascades everywhere by now—and Colin brewed a welcome supper of oxtail soup and bread and mugs of bouillon. When we looked out again it was to see Eiger and Mönch and Jungfrau glittering bright gold in evening sunlight against the background of black cloud, and on the foreground of falling green slopes laced with little streams a large herd of Simmental cows advancing upward to converge upon the tent. They came jangling on until they were ranged in a semicircle a few yards from the doorway, like an operatic chorus, and one of them—the leading lady, doubtless—stepped forward and emitted a powerful and melodious *Mooo!* in our faces.

Colin was impressed. "Listen to that!" he said. "Perfect production—straight from the diaphragm."

As company the Simmentalians were not unwelcome and as vocalists just tolerable; but as campanologists they were a nuisance, choosing 2 a.m. to perform a sort of carillon-pavane round the tent, "every one in their several note", until I burst out into the starlight and dispersed them. Starlight promised a clear morning and the promise was fulfilled. I got breakfast of boiled eggs and tea at 7 in hot sunshine and we ate it sitting on boulders already dry, with the tent steaming in the middle of a ring of admiring cows. So clear was the atmosphere this morning that the snows of the Gspaltenhorn two miles away seemed to rise straight from the verge of our sloping pastures, and the glacier falling from the Silberhorn showed every blue-green crevasse as clearly as through a telescope. By the time we were packed up and away, 9.15, the morning was ominously hot.

A mile of narrow but plain path brought us down to a mountain farm called Bogangen (sleeping-quarters available here) where the way beyond the farm buildings was obscure. A brief trial-and-error discovered the route—a left fork of the path contouring almost level across open mountainside for two miles to turn the Brünli ridge and descend by very steep zigzags into the glen of the Schiltbach. Beyond the hamlet of Gimmeln which lies in the lap of this flowery cwm is the last half-hour of broad and easy track leading into Mürren. The whole of this route is beautiful almost beyond description. You march shoulder-to-shoulder with the rank of 13,000-foot peaks on the other side of the forested trench of the Lauterbrunnen valley, and the path itself, hugging the rim of steep pastures bright with Alpine flowers, doubles round successive corners above a wall of crag and forest.

Mürren, its hotel-lined street car-less and quiet in oppressive heat, provided us with postcards and a new pipe. Perhaps the distant flicker of lightning over the Jungfrau tempted us a little to use the electric railway for a quick transit to the valley 3,000 feet below; but we resisted temptation, and having paused for lunch just beyond Mürren began the long descent by a steep path through the forest. The storm broke upon us when we were halfway down, beginning with a stunning thunderclap and continuing with a deluge that was to last the rest of that day. Dumping the packs under a dripping rock, we tried for half-an-hour to get partial shelter beneath trees and thickets, a vain and futile attempt. Lying in a waterborne tent had given me a nagging rheumatic pain in one shoulder as a result of which I'd been going badly all day, and when we hefted our packs to resume the journey I found that Colin had transferred the tent, which I'd been carrying, to his own load. My protests were in vain. He splashed on down the streaming track and I followed, less painfully now, through the downpour.

Drenched with sweat inside our waterproofs, discharging water at every fold and crease, we crept beneath a pine-tree which the lightning had felled across the path, crossed a wooden bridge that shook with the force of the torrent boiling beneath it, and came down at five o'clock into the main street of Lauterbrunnen. No question of looking for a quiet camp-site here. On past the shops and hurrying umbrellas we marched, heading for the official "Jungfrau" site. A big signboard ushered us into it, a vast place down by the river where neat paths divided blocks of caravans and chalets and buildings. An oilskinned Warden conducted us to a corner between a Dutch caravan and a big frame tent, and five minutes later we had the Itisa pitched and were stripping off our wet things in shelter.

"A bit of a come-down, this," I remarked ungratefully. "And the weather seems to be breaking up."

"It's for heat," said Colin.

6. LAUTERBRUNNEN TO MEIRINGEN

Lauterbrunnen (weatherbound 2 days). Kleine Scheidegg (6,762').
Grindelwald (weatherbound 1 day). Grosse Scheidegg (6,434').
Meiringen. 2 days of walking, 1 wayside camp, 5 camping nights
on official sites.

"This lad from the Rhondda," said Colin, "was bored with

working in the mine and wanted a bit of excitement. Secret
agent for a foreign power was what he thought he'd like, and
after months of sounding his way and secret interviews and
what-have-you he found himself in a pitch-black room receiving
his orders. 'Return to your mine,' says a voice, low and stern.
'In time we shall find work for you. Meanwhile, remember
you have sworn an oath of secrecy.' The Rhondda lad wasn't
best pleased at having to wait. 'Look now, Mister Whosit,'
he says, 'suppose I get the chance of doing some sabotage or
passing on technical information. *Duw!* I'll want to contact
someone, won't I?' The voice seems to be thinking for a minute.
'In the interests of secrecy,' it says at last, 'our agents remain
unknown even to each other. But in extreme urgency you may
act as follows. Go to the house of Dai Jones in Neath Street,
Pontypridd, and say to him *The tide is in at Barry Port.* You will
then receive assistance.'

"Well—back went the Rhondda lad to his mine, and the
days and weeks went on and on without anything happening
until he reckoned planting a bomb under the shop steward
would be better than nothing and he wanted urgently to do
just that. So off he goes on the bus to Neath Street, Pontypridd,
and asks where's Dai Jones's house and they tell him. He
knocks secret-like on the door and a big chap answers it. 'The
tide is in at Barry Port,' says the Rhondda lad in a whisper.
'Wrong house, man,' says the big chap. 'I'm Dai Jones the
insurance. It's next door but two you want—Dai Jones the
spy.' "

After forty-eight hours on the "Jungfrau" camp-site at
Lauterbrunnen my fund of anecdotes was exhausted; but
Colin's was inexhaustible, and in the intervals of eating,
arguing about opera, sleeping, and peering out at the horrible
weather he invariably produced a new one. And outside the
tent a cold rain fell interminably out of the thick grey mist
that flowed like the ghost of a glacier between the vertical walls
of the valley. The Staubbach, most famous of Lauterbrunnen's
waterfalls, was close above the camp-site; the threadlike cascade
which Byron likened to "the pale courser's tail" of the Apoca-
lypse was a short column of white water with its head lost in
the cloud.

The "Jungfrau" site had pretty well everything. There was

a shop, a laundry, showers, a motel and a games room. Our tent was pitched on a prepared camping place where hardcore had been laid and grassed over so that there was good drainage and no mud. There were of course a lot of people using the site, but the place was surprisingly quiet—perhaps because few of the inhabitants stirred out of their caravans, chalets or dormobiles. The three nights we put in here cost the equivalent of £1; expensive camping by our standards but we made all possible use of its facilities, especially the hot water. It had been Sunday, August 13th, when we came down through the storm to Lauterbrunnen, and if we had ignored the bad weather and pushed on over the last two passes we could have reached Meiringen on the 15th and so completed the journey in nineteen days. But it's a poor kind of backpacking that seeks only to finish the journey and cares nothing about missing the fine things to be seen on the way, and the fact that past climbing seasons had taken us both to Kleine Scheidegg before only made us the more anxious not to miss the splendours to be seen from the pass. Hence the two days of waiting for a clearance of the weather. There was not the least sign of clearance on the evening of the second day, but we had had enough of idling in the damp. On August 16th we were away at 7.45 of a dark and dirty morning. We took the signposted path for Wengen (it crosses the river close to the north end of the "Jungfrau" site) and plodded through the foggy drizzle up a broad path zigzagging through forest.

It was a steep fifteen hundred feet to Wengen, a ghost town of apparently deserted hotels looming out of the dripping mist. Here a more open hillside track mounted close to the Wengern Alp rack-and-pinion railway line for the remaining two thousand feet to Kleine Scheidegg. Gone were the towering Eiger, the dazzle of the Eiger Glacier where I'd cut my first steps in ice, the breathtaking face-to-face encounter with the Jungfrau. The ugly buildings of the Jungfraujoch railway station bulking aggressively in the fog might have been at Crewe or Stafford for all the Alpine glamour they suggested. The station restaurant was packed with Japanese tourists, so we ate our bread-and-cheese at one of the wet iron tables on the deserted platform and then went on down the broad and muddy path towards Grindelwald. Out of the gloomy opacity there followed us, as we went, a vast lowing sound suggestive of a Simmental cow with an amplifier. Some indefatigable Swiss was blowing an alpenhorn for the edification of the Japanese; it was part of the show, and in this land of tourism the show must go on.

Today was the twentieth day of our journey and we were nearing its end, though not quite as we had planned. We'd hoped, for instance, to employ our peak-fitness in gaining the summit of the Mannlichen (7,697 feet) two or three miles north along the ridge from Kleine Scheidegg, thence reaching Grindelwald by the hill path descending through Hinter der Egg, a longer alternative but much to be commended in good weather; and we still had a faint hope of getting from Grindelwald to Meiringen by way of a traverse of the Schwarzhorn (9,613 feet), though the map hinted that the descent on the north-east of the peak might be tricky. Both these routes might be considered by anyone backpacking from Lauterbrunnen to Meiringen.

The much-trodden track descending from Kleine Scheidegg on the east curls pleasantly enough down steepening hillsides towards the chalets of Alpiglen, first across slopes of alpenrose and then intermittently through sparse forest. It was odd to be walking so close to a great mountain without the slightest indication that we were doing so. We had looked forward to seeing again that remarkable overhead view of the Eigerwand towering in huge and foreshortened perspective right above the track, but to all appearance there was nothing more than dark mist up there; if any hardy souls were squatting on the Death Bivouac or the Flatiron there was neither sight nor sound of them. We met a herd of aggressively friendly goats and no less than ten people coming up the track, this last a reminder that the largest town in the Oberland was only a couple of hours' walk below us. Unless we wanted another bout of official-site camping we had better start looking for a site below the track. A little short of Alpiglen we found one, but only after half-an-hour's prospecting among the bilberry-clad mounds and rock heaps which are the remains of old rockfalls from the Eigerwand. Once again we got the tent pitched just in time to shelter from a sudden increase of the downpour.

But this last "wild" camp-site wasn't a bad one. True, there was some sort of pylon straddling a rock slab just above, its top invisible; but directly below the tent a stream tumbled in its mossy ravine, eyebright and wild strawberry and bilberry in fruit clothed the hummocks, and Colin was able to indulge his lungs with the operatic arias which compassion for the non-musical had forbidden at Lauterbrunnen. When I got out of the tent in the near-darkness of 8.30 that evening the mist had partly raised its curtain, revealing the huge black base of the Eigerwand rearing vertically, as it seemed, overhead. On the fringe of the mist a point of yellow light glowed steadily—the window of the Jungfraujoch railway that opens in the face of the Wall.

Looking out at the thick mist and steady rain of next morning, we debated whether to make a forced march through Grindel-wald to Meiringen in one day and take the first train home. Colin still thought it was for heat, so we adopted a more leisurely alternative on the hypothesis that five successive days of bad weather would bring back sunshine on the sixth day. We would get down to Grindelwald and give the weather-gods a chance. So, after plodding the rather dull four miles to Grindelwald, we pitched in pouring rain on the "Gletscher" camp-site—one of the four official sites available here—and prepared to sit it out with the help of food, wine, anecdotes, and the new pipe I'd bought in Mürren.

As far as could be seen in this weather, Grindelwald had no surroundings, and without them it has no special beauty. The two sallies we made into its wet and crowded streets for supplies were brief. The "Gletscher" has all the usual facilities of a well-organised site, and when the peaks and glaciers above it are on view it must be a pleasant place enough; but—like the site in Lauterbrunnen, though to a lesser extent—it can only have a limited amount of sunshine because of its position in a deep and narrow valley. I thought nostalgically of the many splendid high camps we had made in the past three weeks of travel, on flower-strewn shelves of the mountainside where the sun was warming the tent before 7 a.m.

Not only was there no sun in the Grindelwald sky, but it was also perishing cold, a circumstance which was explained on the morning of the 18th by the sight of thick new snow on the crags a few hundred feet above the town. With the snowline down to 4,000 feet there was no hope now of bagging the Schwarzhorn on the way to Meiringen. All that day cars and caravans were moving out of the "Gletscher" to go home, "like rats leaving a sinking ship", as Colin said; the now waterlogged camp-site made his comment particularly apt. On the morning of August 19th, the wettest and coldest yet, we joined the rats.

About the wearisome slog up to the Grosse Scheidegg (6,434 feet) the less said the better. A narrow and twisting road, motorable, climbs from Grindelwald to the pass, but its bends can be short-circuited by a direct and stony track. By noon the steady rain had turned to heavy snowfall and on the viewless saddle where the road ended there was two inches of snow underfoot. In all available clothing topped by anoraks and overtrousers we began the descent from our fifteenth and last pass, winding down through a White-Christmassy world. A broad roughly-metalled track led us easily and somewhat depressingly downward; presumably there was to be a motor-road here too, soon. Lower down, the snow ceased and there were glimpses of snowy crags and a glacier at the base of the Wellhorn; and near where we lunched in the shelter of an old saw-mill we picked snow-covered wild raspberries. But these small pleasures were poor compensation for the loss of the vanished Wetterhorn and the fantastic Engelhorner we'd hoped to see when we came down to the green upper valley of Rosen-laui. A road used by cars and motor-coaches begins here, and a notice saying NO CAMPING NO PICNICS confirmed that this was the final descent through conservation into civilisation.

The road, descending in hairpin bends beside a torrent, bored us after a mile or two and I suggested escaping on to a footpath on the left, where one of the two people we met on this route, a Swiss workman, assured us that we should reach Meiringen by going this way. So we did, and with heartening close-up views of the spectacular Reichenbach Fall into which Sherlock Holmes and Moriarty the master-criminal fell locked in each other's arms. But the path ended at the gateway of the funicular railway by which the fall is reached from the valley, and since there was no other way of continuing the descent on foot we finished the twenty-three-day journey as we had begun it, by rail.

Meiringen is a pleasant little town even in the rain, and its

Tourist Information Office is kindly disposed towards drenched and dripping backpackers. They found us quarters at four francs a night in the roomy loft of Meiringen school, a place used on occasion by detachments of Switzerland's conscript army, where there were foam-rubber mattresses and plenty of room to dry out wet clothes and tent. The caretaker spoke no English and we were uncertain whether or not we were allowed to light our stove, so Colin cooked supper in the toilet while I kept watch. Over supper we cheered ourselves by doing a summing-up of the journey. We had crossed fifteen passes, ascending in all 40,337 feet and descending 39,953 feet; we had had seventeen days of fair weather and seven of foul; we had seen more of the Swiss mountain scene than either of us had done on previous Alpine holidays; and the cost amounted to £48 each, £39 of which was train and boat fare. Moreover, we were physically fitter than we had been for some years; fit to go on backpacking indefinitely in fact.

"Wire home," suggested Colin. "Unavoidably detained. Then we go on eastward—Glarus Alps, Vorarlberg, Tyrol."

"In weather like this?"

"It's for heat—I keep telling you," said Colin, and this time he was right.

Next day (our train didn't leave Interlaken until evening) we toiled in blazing sunshine up to the little village of Reuti on its mountain-shelf above Meiringen. Beyond the green Aar valley at our feet the Oberland mountains tossed their white crests joyously into blue sky. The sharp-pointed Schwarzhorn which we had hoped to traverse was as dazzling-white as the Wetterhorn with new snow, and the Engelhorner lifted red-and-white pinnacles like the tines of a giant's rake above the gorge of the Reichenbach down which we had come yesterday. The Grosse Scheidegg was hidden and all our other passes were far beyond the western horizon. But we were well content. All that we had seen on the uncounted miles of our journey was safely stored in memory, to be unrolled like a precious tapestry in years to come.

TWO

The Central Pyrenees

1. AX TO PORTA

Ax-les-Thermes. Forges d'Orlu. Porteille de la Grave (8,020').
"Nameless Pass" (?8,000'). Etang de Lanoux. Porté. Porta.
2½ days, 3 camps.

Four of us disembarked from the trans-France night train at
Ax-les-Thermes in the brilliant sunshine of seven o'clock on a
morning in late July. This was the year following the Oberland
journey just described, and Colin Morgan and I had enlisted
reinforcements for a four-week exploration of the Central
Pyrenees—Jim Thomas, a burly north-countryman, and Brad-
ford Herzog, a gigantic professional photographer from
Massachusetts. The average age of this backpacking party
was 53.

It's easy to get to the Pyrenees from London. The French
railway comes very close to the frontier range at two places,
Ax-les-Thermes and Bagnères de Luchon, and from Ax (and
less pleasantly from Luchon) you can walk straight into the
mountains and be in the Pyrenean solitudes less than 24 hours
after leaving Victoria. Which makes it all the stranger that
information about travel on foot in the Pyrenees is very hard to
come by. French and Spanish tourist offices will send you stacks
of pamphlets describing the skiing, sunbathing, riding and night-
life of Pyrenean resorts and there is now a somewhat unsatis-
factory guidebook in English to the rock-climbing. My
researches proved that Belloc's *The Pyrenees*, published in 1909
and long out-of-date on such matters as roads and inns, is still
the best book for the walker or backpacker anxious to discover
in advance what sort of country he is likely to encounter on a
journey.

As the only one of us who had been to the Pyrenees before—
I'd done a fortnight's walking there 39 years ago—I was

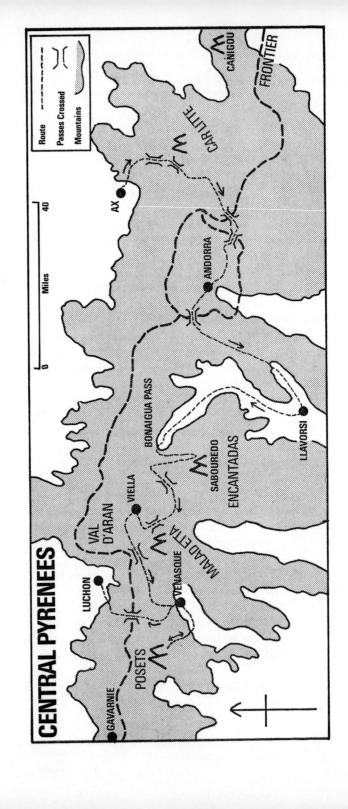

responsible for planning a route. Maps (see Appendix A) were difficult to obtain and those of the Spanish side where most of our time would be spent were lacking in detail and sometimes inaccurate, but this only added to the pleasant suspicion, later to be confirmed, that Pyrenean backpacking was going to be much more of a pioneering venture than last year's Oberland trek. The central part of the range holds the highest and most interesting peaks and ridges, but the many long spurs jutting southward into Spain invited exploration. To make the most of our four weeks, I decided, we ought to make two if not three "raids" to the south from our line of march along the frontier ridge; starting from Ax and finishing at Luchon for the homeward train, we could achieve something like 200 miles of mountain wandering by discarding the original scheme of traversing east-to-west along the main range, and see more and remoter mountains. This plan we followed, and I recommend it to other backpackers.

My route-planning was influenced by two other things. One was Colin's insistence on entering Andorra, which once remote little country is now the haunt of French tourists driving into it by the busy main road over the Col de Puymorens; to avoid this road I proposed to start eastward from Ax and cross the wild mountain region called the Carlitte, thence coming into Andorra over two little-known passes. The other thing was my own wish to make the final re-crossing into France by the 9,655-foot Port d'Oo, to see whether my reactions to this wildest of passes would be the same as in 1934. The start and finish of the journey were thus fairly clear in our minds and the rest of it fairly hazy as we set out from Ax at 11 o'clock, our packs distended with the three days' supplies bought in the little town's well-stocked market.

For fifteen minutes the going was hell. It was Saturday, we were on the main road to Andorra, and the midday sun beat upon us from a cloudless sky. An endless chain of cars zipped past, each discharging a puff of dust on our single-file pack train. But only for fifteen minutes. The left-turn on the lane signposted ORLU brought us at once into quieter country with no traffic, and the scenery quickly became exciting—blue forest soaring above the river-valley to end at the base of spectacular crags. Beyond the two or three stone houses of

3

Forges d'Orlu the lane became a stony track bordered with flowery thickets, and the occasional painful encounter with horseflies was a small price to pay for the sight of the narrowing valley-walls framing the buttressing shoulders of unseen mountains ahead. Our aim on this first half-day was merely to reach a place where we could camp "wild", so when at four o'clock we came to a delightful spot between wood and river, where an old mule-bridge crossed the river (the Oriège) and the track beyond climbed more steeply, the word was "off packs and pitch".

The Itisa tent so well proven in the Oberland housed Colin and me. Jim and Brad had a tent each, small ridge-tents of a size just adequate to Jim's bulk but not to Brad's length. Brad protruded. This meant that the bottom of his magnificent American sleeping-bag was always damp, which was a little hard on a man who was making his first backpacking trip; but Brad never complained, and merely chuckled when it was discovered that the inflatable "Surfrider" which Colin and I had used as a mattress in the Oberland only insulated a small part of his frame from the ground.

Romantic memories of that Pyrenean journey of forty years ago had led me to ordain that stoves should be left behind and all cooking done on wood fires; and from now on I was—justly —regarded as responsible for producing a pot-worthy fire at evening and morning. The wood of the Oriège thickets was damp, but the clouds of smoke from our first camp-fire were at least helpful in repelling the midges and did in the end result in flames and hot soup. Tea, soup and potato mash, and biscuits was our dinner that evening, with jam and new-baked bread for anyone who needed "afters". Darkness comes early here, more than 600 miles south of London, and it seemed natural to turn in at a quarter to nine, after (an invariable and invaluable precaution) I had placed some dry wood for the morning in the empty fireplace and covered it with a slab of rock. The companionable mumble of the river continued when our sleeping-bag conversations had ended and greeted us when we woke next morning; it was to be the same at most of our Pyrenean camps. With a boiled egg and bread and jam inside us, we were packed and away at 8.30 of a dull and mercifully cool morning.

One of several recent books about the Pyrenees I had read,

unprofitably for our purpose, had dismissed the Carlitte as a region of rounded hills. Flagrant misrepresentation is a mild term for this description. Toiling up the steep mule-track, with an increasingly chill wind to prevent overheating, we climbed through a corridor of spiky peaks into a superb amphitheatre of snow-streaked crags and aspiring ridges. All the way up we had been passing masses of flowers—pink dianthus grew everywhere —and now, in this wild corrie holding the Lac de Beys, we came to the Alpines, androsacae and gentian perched among the grey boulders with many others. Nothing I'd read about the Pyrenees had prepared me for the wealth of flora that greeted us throughout our journey. Near the lake there is the ruin of an old Refuge, and here we encountered the only other walkers we saw on that day or the next—four young French climbers. They could tell us nothing about the route to the Porteille de la Grave, the 8,000-foot pass we were aiming for, and since the French half-inch map we were using was singularly unhelpful we had to rely on compass and common sense for the afternoon's manoeuvres. And it's worth repeating that a compass *and* common sense are vital adjuncts to the map in Pyrenean travel.

A small but impassable rock-bluff closed in the head of the lake, no path was discoverable. Over a chaos of great rocks where alpenrose grew with bilberry and heather we clambered, bypassing the bluff until we could traverse back to the left on to the steep boulder-slope mounting towards the pass. There might possibly (we thought afterwards) be an easier route farther to the left. Our chosen line involved tricky route-finding up vegetated ledges and not a little hand-and-foot work. There was one moment on an awkward corner when I thought that Brad, whose mighty pack-frame increased his overall height to well over seven feet, would surely peel off and go cartwheeling down to the lake. But a last near-impasse up which Jim pioneered a slippery route brought us over an abrupt rim to a little black tarn. Just visible above and beyond, under the ragged fringes of lowering cloud, were screes and rock-ribs streaked with snow—the final rise to the Porteille.

A problem common enough in this sort of backpacking now confronted us. It was only half-past two. The col we had to cross was a thousand feet above us, a hard climb but not more than

1½ hours away, and we had no idea how long it would take us to get down to water and a camp-site on the other side. The rim on which we had arrived was flat enough for tents and the lake water was handy, but the place was exposed to a strong cold wind. Should we press on, taking a chance on the gathering mists and the finding of a camp-site before dark? Or should we make the best of our present position? The vote went three to one in favour of staying put; a wise decision, I thought. While the others pitched the three flapping tents I built a fire of juniper twigs and battled with the harrying wind to produce a brew of tea. Even here, at 7,000 feet, there was adequate fuel when the sparse juniper was supplemented with alpenrose roots and at 6 we ate a reasonable supper based on soup and more tea, for the cooking of which I built a more sheltered fireplace under the rocky bank that held in the tarn. By 8 we were all in our sleeping-bags.

Camp Two was romantically sited, as on a stage. Like the wings of a disproportionate proscenium, shattered precipices soared into the mists on either hand, and where the auditorium would have been was the almost sheer drop into the vast corrie whence we had climbed, with the crags of its opposite side beyond. For backdrop we had the cloud-capped buttresses of bony crags with the gloomy tarn between their feet, and the pass, now lost to sight, above it. It was not typical of our Pyrenean camps, though. Nor was the Porteille de la Grave a typical Pyrenean "port".

We were away at 8.15 on a cloudy morning that showed a hint of brightness in the mists overhead. There was no track, no sign at all that anyone had passed that way before. By very steep boulder-slopes, by slanting ribbons of snow and a final easy hand-and-foot clamber, we came to the narrow crest of the pass—1 hour and 20 minutes from the camp-site. And here, in that moment, the clouds blew clear away and we were in brilliant sunshine. At our feet as we lolled among the spiky boulders the eastern flank of the pass fell very steeply for perhaps 2,000 feet into a wide and empty river-valley where cloud-shadows moved and slowly climbed the heights of hill and forest. As far as the eye could see—and we looked across some thirty or forty square miles—the landscape was completely unmarked by Man. Prospecting by the more impatient members of the party revealed that there was no trace of a downward track on the east. We were delighted.

"This is beyond all expectation," said Jim contentedly. "I'd not have believed there was still pioneering to be done in Europe. If it's like this all the way—"

But it wasn't, quite. The Pyrenees had greater wonders, more splendid scenery, in store for us; but not again (except on parts of the Port d'Oo crossing) did we exert our route-finding craft so continuously, or feel so strongly that we were in an untrodden mountain sanctuary, as we did on the Porteille de la Grave.

Route-finding was needed the moment we shouldered packs and started down, and compass-work too. The Porteille was like a sally-port in the east wall of the Carlitte fortress and we had still to keep within the bounds of the fortress in order to make our exit by the main south-western gate—the long valley leading down to the village of Porté on the main road from Ax into Spain. The route now led southward along the face of the wall, as it were, to a breach in its castellations through which we could reach the head of this valley. The second pass was nameless on our map, and to reach it a slanting descent was necessary below the crags on our right to gain the ascending glen or ravine on our left. We were getting used to adjusting balance to the top-heavy packs, which was just as well because the footing on the slope was none too good. Reaching easier ground a few hundred feet above the ravine, we could look up to its head and see the nameless pass, a saddle between the Pic de La Grave on the north and the ridges of the Pic Carlitte massif on the south, with a thousand feet of steep but not difficult ascent leading straight up to it. Across on the other side of the ravine there was something that might be a path, but between us and it was a gully filled with crags and topped by a snowslope, so we held to our line and sweated (a foretaste of many sweatings to come) up the rocky bluffs and shaly screes to the col.

The illusion of a primal land unvisited until our arrival vanished at a stroke here; though the stroke was a mere yellow line two miles away. Ahead the gentlest of grassy slopes spread down into a spacious plateau hemmed in by rock-peaks golden in the noonday sun, with a long blue lake stretching along the feet of the western peaks—a lake whose farther shore was marked by the perfectly straight band of yellow shale that indicated a man-made reservoir at summer level. The Etang de Lanoux (*etang* or *estang* is Pyrenean patois for lake) has a high dam at its south-western end, for hydro-electric power. But the dam was out of sight round a corner of cliff far ahead, and the scene was really too beautiful to be spoiled by mere knowledge of its existence. On the broad crest of the col was another sign of civilisation, a small cairn and a worn waymark of red paint; this pass, in fact, links Porté to Les Angles and Formiguères in the upper Aude valley, though it is seldom used. The path that took us downward towards the lake was faint and intermittent, and the high-watermark of the lake was the only other trace of human life.

When we were nearly at the lake shore we could look back at the impressive barrier we had crossed by our two passes. The Pic de la Grave, a fine rock summit, rises from the jagged ridge, and we had steered a zigzag course round it by using the Porteille and the "nameless" pass. A more direct route had been discussed: to steer south-south-west from the tarn where we had camped (Etang de la Grave) and cross the Col de Lanoux, which would have brought us straight down to the big lake. The south side of this col was now in view, and we could see that it was steep and rocky—fun, perhaps, for the hardy scrambler but not for the laden backpacker.

The path, such as it was, became positively idyllic when it began to skirt the shore of the lake. The compact massif of the Pic Carlitte, 9,700 feet, sends down its ridges to end in rocky buttresses above the waters of Lanoux, and the clefts between them are miniature paradises of greensward and flowers and tumbling bright streams. In and out of these dells wound the path and in one of them we halted for lunch and a rest. A little earlier we had glimpsed the attractive inner glens between the ridges, each of them inviting exploration and promising good mountaineering.

"You could camp here for a fortnight and do a different climb or scramble every day," said Colin.

It was a comment made times without number during our progress through these delectable mountains.

Just short of the dam at the lake's end we came upon the

first people we had seen that day, a party of ten or twelve tourists lunching. The dam glowered impressively above a magnificent gorge, and the path, dipping to cross the head of the gorge, became for the next mile or so a regular cliff-hanger skirting its northern rim. It was half-past three when we rounded a high corner and saw a motorable lane far below us in the valley bottom, and a lake with the tiny figures of anglers standing round it. Two miles beyond, the houses of Porté could be seen where this side valley debouched into the wider valley carrying the main road. Across the larger glen rose a complex of high ridges, black-crested against the glare of the westering sun: the mountain frontier of Andorra.

We had planned to camp well short of Porté and stock up there on the morrow for a three-camp journey to Andorra la Vella, the little country's capital. Already Porté was too close for comfort, for there was no tent site nor any water on the steep mountainside traversed by our path and the lane to which we must descend was dotted with parked cars and strolling tourists. "Make camp too soon rather than too late" is a sound motto for the solitude-loving backpacker descending into civilisation from the wilds. But in the event things proved better than they looked. An awkward descent on a declivity of thorns and stones brought us to the car-haunted lane, a bridge of planks took us across the river that ran beside it, and after a brief search we found a site close to the stream where the flat and stony ground was screened from the lane by thorn-bushes. By the time the customary first brew-up was ready (billy boiled in ten minutes, fire lit with one match and no paper) the cars had departed and all was peace. The only creature we saw after that was an adder, discovered when I up-ended a flat rock for the improvement of my fireplace; when I stirred it up with the end of a stick it struck once and then wriggled away into the bushes. Adders are not aggressive when left to their own devices, and we slept none the less soundly for the knowledge of their presence. But there was a certain amount of cautious prying round the edges of tents next morning.

A splendid morning it was when at ten o'clock (late, but we had shaved) we came down the lane into Porté, a Pyrenean hamlet with modern additions designed to convert it into a fashionable winter sports centre. There was a somewhat tatty restaurant where we indulged in coffee and rolls at exorbitant prices, but no *épicerie*. For groceries, they told us, we would have to go on to Porta, two-and-a-half kilometres down the main road which came coiling down the mountainside a few hundred yards beyond the village. Since the mule track leading to our next pass started from Porta this posed no problem. Girding up our shorts-clad loins, we plunged in single file into the dust and heat of Route Nationale 20.

Fortunately that one-and-a-half miles in near-tropical heat, with cars hooting past us every thirty seconds, was all down-hill. And Porta when we came to it was a more than compensatory delight. This tiny unspoilt Pyrenean village has been bypassed by the busy Col de Puymorens road, and its narrow black-shadowed alleys, its crowded rough-stone dwellings with geraniums flaming under the iron grilles of the windows, and its atmosphere of dung and antiquity, were like a soothing balm after the brash pseudo-modernity of Porté. Here I exercised my rusty French in an *épicerie* that might have been round the corner from Goblin Market. There was no shop window, no indication that anything at all was sold in the tiny house. You went in through a green-painted door that was certainly no more than five feet high, and down several worn stone steps (the rooms were three feet below ground level) to find yourself in a dimly-lit living room with nothing in it but furniture. A door led out of this into the shop, surprisingly roomy and stocked with all the things we needed—packet soups, bread, eggs, and a bottle of local wine which cost 2 francs 50, about five shillings. To replenish my supply of pipe tobacco I had to enter another apparently private house, this time climbing the stairs to an upper living room where the house-holder was taking wine with two *gendarmes*. Packets of the dry, fast-burning *régie* tobacco were produced from a wall cupboard at my demand. I seized the opportunity of asking the *gendarmes* how we should get our passports stamped when we entered Andorra by a mountain pass; this was a question that had been worrying Jim, who as a Customs and Excise official had inside knowledge of what happened to travellers who failed to conform to regulations. The answer was that passports were only stamped at the road frontiers and our best course was to report our arrival in Andorra to the *gendarmerie* there. Thus advised, and with the food and wine distributed equally by weight among our bulging packs, we drank a pint of milk each from bottles and set off for Andorra.

2. PORTA TO ANDORRA LA VELLA

Porta. Portella Blanca d'Andorra (8,364'). Col de l'Illa (9,025'). Upper Madriu valley. Andorra la Vella. 2½ days. 2 camps, 1 bivouac.

From Porta we had only to cross the main road and walk a hundred yards up a lane on the other side to be free of petrol fumes and breathing flower-scented mountain air again. The heat of early afternoon dropped on us like a tangible weight as the lane became a mule-track and began to climb very steeply, rounding a corner below some fine crags that guarded the entrance to the valley of Campcardos. This was a characteristic Pyrenean mule-track, centuries old and now little used by mules or anything else, laboriously paved with big round stones set close together—harassing to feet in vibram-soled boots but presumably acceptable to the hooves of pack animals. At its foot there was a thicket of tall hazels below the tumbledown wall on its outer edge, and I halted here to cut a staff to replace the makeshift one that had accompanied me from our first camp by the Oriège.

The others were out of sight when I started up the track again. The way curled upward into a very beautiful valley flanked by noble rock-peaks whose bases rose from sunlit thickets where a torrent flashed whitely. There were multitudes of flowers everywhere, tall pale-blue campanulas and purple gentians among them, with unidentifiable butterflies of twice normal size and dazzling colours flapping lazily between them. Higher up, the deep pink dianthus which struggles in tiny clumps in my Welsh garden grew in great glowing cushions. The mule-track ceased to be paved and walled after an hour or so and continued as a mere trace of passage, threading an ever-mounting way into a mountain wilderness that seemed never to have been tamed. It was the more surprising to meet three people coming down the path, two men and a woman,

3*

with whom I exchanged brief greetings. By their rusty-black clothes, as also by the brown leathery skins and curious accent, they were Pyreneans, and their easy swinging stride as they went on down the track made my own slow progress upward feel doubly arduous.

But the angle eased quite soon. I came up with the rest of the party and we topped a rise to enter an almost level basin floored with grass and flowers. All about it stood grand rock-peaks eight or nine thousand feet high, with little streams flashing and leaping down from the couloirs between them to the marshy verges of a small lake. The basin was a typical Pyrenean *jasse*. A second steep rise led out of it to a higher and barer glen at the far end of which, about two thousand feet above us, a nick between descending skyline ridges gleamed strangely white against the blue sky. The nick could only be the Portella Blanca, the Little White Gate of Andorra.

It was four o'clock and this time there was no argument about going on. We pitched the tents in this delectable place. "There are no such pipes to be smoked as those that follow a good day's march"—and if Stevenson had been more of a tea-drinker he would have added "and no such cuppas to be drunk". Brad (who had once taught Eng. Lit. in a Massachusetts academy) would have disagreed, for he was no smoker and preferred his tea unflavoured with juniper smoke. But it was Brad who always collected the firewood for that first brew-up, departing with gigantic strides into the middle distance and returning like Birnam Wood coming to Dunsinane, so lengthy and massive were the boughs he carried. He could never understand why we didn't have a "proper" camp-fire instead of my mingy little affairs of twigs in an eight-inch-square fireplace built of rocks; but in long-ago days when I was tramping Europe I had learned that the small contained fire is the easiest to manipulate, the least wicked at burning the cook's fingers, and the fastest for a quick brew if the wood is Best Selected, which is to say absolutely dry. There was plenitude of wood at all our Pyrenean sites and at more than one of them Brad was to have his heart's desire in the way of a good blaze.

"*A super supper*," comments my Log. "*Two different packet soups, bread, tin of apple purée bought in Porta, and wine.*" The enthusiasm reads oddly divorced from its context of mountain air, strenuous load-carrying, and a lunch consisting merely of bread, cheese, and half a tomato. Perhaps the magnificent scenery around us also played its part in turning a frankly uninteresting meal into a gourmet's feast. It was a piquant sauce to soup and bread, as we sat eating outside in the warm sunshine that still sufficiently tempered a cold breeze, to gaze at soaring crests and rock-ribs whose bases were only a five-minute scramble away and debate whether they were climbable —and whether anyone had ever tried to climb them. It was another of the spots where a week's camping and exploring would not exhaust the possibilities. When we left it next morning, in hot sunshine after a remarkably cold night, I for one felt unreasonably guilty, as a man might do who has deliberately spurned a generous offer that will not be made again.

In the upper *jasse* of the Campcardos glen there were more peaks, all eminently climbable; the highest of these was about 9,600 feet and we saw no snow on them. Nor did we see any chamois, though the region we had been crossing for the past four days is supposed to abound in them. Flowers, indeed, were again multitudinous, especially the purple gentian, but I spotted only one solitary star-shaped bloom of the blue spring gentian so common in the Alps. Flowers and turf gave place to knobbly scree which thinned higher up to shale almost as fine as gravel, set at no very high angle. The foot-wide path, none too clear in places, mounted easily to a final slope of white scree forming the saddle of the pass. We pushed through the Little White Gate of Andorra, 8,364 feet above the sea.

But—not into Andorra. The Portella Blanca stands at the apex of a right-angled corner which the Andorran frontier thrusts eastward into France, and from this same apex the frontier between France and Spain drops a few miles southward before turning east. Three nations, two big and one very small, thus meet on the pass and an obelisk of hewn stone marks the exact place of their meeting. (Walking briskly round the obelisk, you pass in a few seconds from a Republic through a Totalitarian State into a Mediaeval Seigneury.) For our purpose, the descent from the Portella straight into Andorra was impracticable. For one thing, it was not straight but far otherwise, the route fetching a wide compass to the northward before making any westerly headway and in doing so crossing a succession of mountain slopes involving a great deal of up and down; for another, when it did at last enter the main valley where Andorra la Vella stands it joined the main road a dozen miles from the capital. It was altogether to our advantage to go down south-westward into Spain and keep on that side of the frontier for a few miles—following, as it were, the underside of Andorra's right-angled projection—and then climb up north-westward to cross a second pass, the Port de Vall Civera, into Andorra. The descent from this looked a long one but it was at least notably shorter than the alternative and would bring us into Andorra la Vella without any walking on motor-roads. We took a last look at the tangle of ridges and unidentifiable summits stretching southward into the noonday haze and started down into Spain.

A reasonable track wound its way down the gully of a small stream, between craggy slopes that soon sprouted stunted pines. The stream was the youthful Riu de la Llosa, a tributary of the Ebro, and if we had followed it for 150 miles or so we would have passed through the city of Lerida and reached the Mediterranean eighty miles from Barcelona. Its noisy torrent was beside us for rather less than 2,000 feet of descent, as far as a charming dell of grass and trees where two side-streams joined the southbound Llosa, one from the east and one from the west. Our route to the next pass was up the latter.

If the map hadn't assured us we were in Spain I think we would have guessed it from the heat. It *felt* Spanish. It breathed the word "siesta" in that sun-filled windless dell, and crouching in the shade of the trees that overhung the Vall Civera stream we rested, lunched, and smoked beyond our usual halting-time. At 1.30 we started up again, somewhat sluggishly, on a good path that climbed steadily for two miles above the true left bank of the stream and dwindled to a doubtful trace when it reached two small lakes. Possibly because we were too hot to bother we didn't look at the map; the pass, or its whereabouts, could be seen plainly enough above—a long undulating ridge slung between two sharp peaks—and we had only to go straight up by the easiest route. In fact, the proper route crosses to the right bank of the stream about a quarter of a mile below the lakes, and we were too far to the north. Fatigue may have led us into this piece of carelessness. We were all tired, myself especially, and though it was only three o'clock I cast away pride and suggested making camp here.

"It's an ideal site," I urged. "Nearly as good as last night's. And it looks on the map as if water's a long way down on the other side."

But I was outvoted three to one. In vain I cited the good backpacker's rule never to pass a really good camping place after three in the afternoon. In vain (waxing warmer) I hinted that a more suitable pass for my companions was one farther south called the Col dels Clots. We pressed on, led by Jimmy, up an extremely steep and toilsome mountainside, following illusory little paths which vanished maddeningly whenever a crag or ravine interrupted progress—a pretty sure sign that they had been made by chamois. We were halfway up this slope when, looking across to the left, we made out the thread-like line of the path we should have been on, mounting at an easier angle to the obvious lowest point of the saddle a mile away to southward. No one ventured the superfluous comment. It would have been futile to try to cross the intervening steeps of crag and shale so we laboured on and eventually gained the crest, a notch between two airy knife-edges of rock, at four o'clock.

The map, belatedly produced, told us that we were on the Col de l'Illa, 9,025 feet, so we were crossing a pass 300 feet higher than the one we had set out to cross. It was late in the day to be that high; in the Pyrenees comfortable sites with wood and water laid on are usually found at about the 6,000-foot contour, not higher.

" '*Rifugi*'," muttered Colin, reading the map. "Two dots by the cluster of lakes at twenty-three hundred metres. How high's that in feet?"

"Seven thousand five hundred." Jim was looking over his shoulder. "Only fifteen hundred feet down and right on our route."

"Wa-a-l!" Brad produced his best Boston drawl. "Why don't we roost in these same *rifugi*?"

It was agreed. We had read of the Refuges, huts of wood or stone sparsely scattered throughout the Pyrenees, and it would be amusing to sample one as well as convenient to the late hour and our weariness. The descent was straightforward and not unduly steep, due west from the Col de l'Illa. There was no path, but the largest of the three lakes shown on the map was in full view and in less than an hour we were down by its marshy shore and following a plain track. We passed the *rifugi*, a couple of large wooden hovels, without investigating their interiors; the ground round them was filthy with ancient litter and rotting food, and they stank. The sun was dipping towards the crests of the mountains but a path went on south-westward and so did we.

I had seized the opportunity of the halt on the pass to fortify myself with four dextrosol tablets, and whether on this account or because it was all downhill now I was in the lead and skipping like a he-goat. (In my experience dextrosol, glucose in its purest form, has a fast and very noticeable booster effect when the body's natural resources are at a low ebb; it works with Senior Citizens as well as with the commonalty.) There were several immature paths leading away from the dirty Refuge and we had chosen the one that headed most southerly, since the upper Madriu valley we were now heading for was south of us, running east and west. It was a trail that would have puzzled Chingachgook. The lakes occupied a wide marshy shelf of the mountains, a charming place if it hadn't been for the Refuge, and the outer rim of the shelf was formed of picturesque rocky bluffs dropping to the valley. The path, so faint as to be quite indistinguishable to any eye but that of faith, twisted and swerved to dodge between the rocks and the waters of a second lake and at length made a right-angle turn due north. At this point I gave it up and plunged down a gully leading south, landing myself in a series of hazards on crumbling screes and in a small pinewood that somehow managed to exist on the face of a precipice. The others wisely held on with the path and found that it eventually merged with a plainer track. All the same, I was the first to burst through a thorny thicket and slither down into the flower-sprinkled grasses of an upland paradise.

If our pressing on over the Col de l'Illa needed any justification this was it. The first steep descent of the Madriu from its springs on the mountainside above was checked here in a flat oval of yellow grassland cradled in mossy rocks, under the more aloof protection of bold rock-peaks that rose in corrie and spire a mile to the southward. The little river rippled in blue-and-gold coils along the south side of the glen close under a low wall of slabs and boulders, at one place leaving a dozen yards of level dry turf between rock and stream. It was the perfect camp-site (though we were to hail several others as perfect later on) and we had the tents up there at once. Andorra had welcomed us with the gift of a jewel.

As usual, the place had the air of primeval peace undisturbed, but there were three residents to dispel the illusion—a family of mare, foal, and stallion, beautiful animals who could certainly not be ownerless. They stared and stamped and snorted on the other side of the stream while we ate our supper, a picture of rare beauty—I mean, of course, the horses—with their glossy skins and tossing manes golden in the evening sun-light. After sunset and washing-up I lit a pipe and strolled to the western end of the level basin, only a few hundred yards away, and from a dome of rock looked down above the tops of the falling pines into the blue-black gorge of the Madriu. The pine-feathered mountainsides that enclosed its windings stood in sharp silhouette against a glowing sky of palest orange, and more distantly, above an intervening gulf filled with purple haze, another mountain silhouette ran jaggedly against the glow. By turning my back on it I could look up to the eastern frontier of Andorra which we had just crossed; and that distant opposing crest of eleven straight miles away was its western frontier. The little country has an area of only 188 square miles so it isn't remarkable that one can see across it from side to side. But somehow it added to the enchantment. A chill wind came hissing up through the pines and sent me back to the tents for a 9 o'clock turn-in.

One surprising thing about Pyrenean backpacking was the great variation between day and night temperatures. There had been moderately hot days and moderately cold nights at similar heights in the Bernese Oberland, but in the Spanish Pyrenees the qualifying word was not "moderately" but "very". When I got out of the tent next morning after a cold night in all available wrappings there was a white frost on the grass. However, by half-past eight a hot sun had dried the tents and we were stripped to the waist for the various chores of striking camp, which as always included a final effort devoted to restoring our site to its original un-camped-on appearance. While we were at it the owner of the horses came up from the gorge path bridle in hand. He was a broad, stocky Andorran with a walnut-shell face, and in the course of a conversation in halting French he told us that it was two hours down to Andorra la Vella. As he left us to climb the valley towards the three brown specks at its upper end, we opined that he must be intending to ride down; for the map distance was ten miles. But from the moment we left our idyllic glen and plunged into the gorge it was clear that even Turpin, or that nameless rider from Ghent to Aix, would have had to lead his horse down the path.

The path down the Madriu lingers in memory as the most beautiful river-glen walk I've ever done. By steep forest and flower-strewn glades, by ravines close to the glitter of waterfalls and cliff corners poised above them, a very rough but plain track brought us steadily down through brilliant sunlight and stippled shade. We met no one in the three hours it took to reach the second of the two *bordas* marked on the map. A *borda* (the Spanish maps abbreviate it to "B.") is a small hamlet or large farm. Both the *bordas* on the upper Madriu were deserted, their little stone-walled fields turned to wasteland; the mountain-dwelling peasant, like the muleteer, has almost vanished from the Andorran scene, departed to the easier life of the valleys. The next stage, predictably, will be the reoccupation of the *bordas* by holidaying families from Lerida or Barcelona. Near the foot of the valley path we found something of this kind taking place, where some young French folk on holiday were roosting in a couple of old buildings in the forest thickets; theirs was a very peaceful retreat, but their presence was a sign that we were nearly down to civilisation again. Twenty minutes on down the path a high corner gave a sight of power lines and rooftops in the deep valley beyond.

It was at this point that the rain began. The heat of the day had intensified as we came lower down the gorge, and slowly the sky had clouded over. Now a growl of thunder and a spatter of big drops warned of a drenching to come. I was in the rear as we put on speed to seek shelter, and I pounded round a steep bend to see Jim gesticulating from the upper

"Camp Two" at about 7,000 feet, below the Porteille de la Grave

Noris; a Pyrenean hamlet almost, but not quite, deserted

Étang de Mig, looking towards the Cirque de Sabouredo

Summit of the Port Vell de Viella (8,182 feet). Maladetta massif in distance, top right

The old Bridge of Cuberre

Crossing the Port d'Oo (9,655 feet) by the wrong route. Start of the descent into France

window-opening of a ruined barn below the track. We were all in shelter when the spatter turned suddenly to a deluge.

The old stone building was romantically perched among thickets above a steep boulder-slope, and on investigation (an hour's downpour gave us ample time to investigate) proved to be reasonably clean and free from insect and reptile life. A few holes in the roof let in the rain but a few holes in the wooden floor let it out again into the windowless lower storey, and there was enough sound flooring to provide room for four sleeping-bags. Since the barn could not be more than half-an-hour above Andorra la Vella it would make a convenient base. The resolution to make it our quarters for the night was unanimous. At 4 the rain stopped and the sun burst out again, drying the dripping thickets almost instantaneously. Carefully hiding our packs in a *cache* among the thickets, we sallied down into the city by a route of little paths which brought us finally down stone steps between the houses to the long main street—and disenchantment.

Recollection shies away from Andorra la Vella as it is today. Forty years ago I had tramped into it from the mountains and found it a tiny delightful place with a dusty central *plaza* where a few mules slumbering in the sun and some black-clad women washing clothes in a stone trough were the only visible inhabitants. Now it was an ugly inferno of noise, heat, stink, and traffic. Hideous concrete buildings, nearly all either cheapjack souvenir shops or stores selling duty-free goods, flanked a mile and a half of crowded pavements, between which an endless double line of automobiles moved at 2 m.p.h. or less, exuding an unbearable miasma of petrol fumes. The mountains still looked down, serrated and beautiful, on the central *plaza*; but the *plaza* was now a traffic jam surrounded by bus stops and ice-cream stalls. The fumes from the hundreds of crawling cars were worse than anything I'd experienced in the streets of London or Manchester and affected me for the first time in my life; only a beer in a timely *taverna*, I think, saved me from fainting. After the beer I was sufficiently recovered to pursue a *gendarme* and ask him where the *gendarmerie* was, so that we could get our passports stamped and regularise our entry. He pointed out the *gendarmerie* and said they were far too busy there to bother with passports. So we stocked up hurriedly in a supermarket, snatched a passable meal in a café, and toiled back heavy-laden up the steps and paths to our peaceful ruin. We had had enough of Andorra the Old, now Andorra the Horrible.

That was a quiet night of sound sleep, on the hard old planks with the rustle of the torrent coming in through the frameless window. Breakfast next morning was supplemented by the big wild raspberries that grew on the steeps below the barn. In clear hot sunshine we made a leisurely descent once more into Andorra la Vella, this time intent on getting away from it as far and as fast as possible.

Inquiry had revealed that a bus left at 1 p.m. for Arinsal, a village six miles on our way out towards Spain. The crowd in the bus received the entrance of ourselves and our packs goodhumouredly despite the damage to their knees and toes, the vehicle hooted its way into the car-queue, and we heaved a sigh of relief as the streets of the capital were left behind. So far as I could see, Progress had brought only one good thing to Andorra la Vella—a public lavatory as magnificent as any in London or Paris.

3.   ANDORRA LA VELLA TO SABOUREDO

Andorra. Port Vell (8,203'). Llavorsi. Port de Bonaigua (road pass). Cirque de Sabouredo. 4½ days, 4 camps.

There is an exaggerative effect in sudden contrast like the effect of the microphone that turns the pop singer's wail into a stunning howl. Plain water tastes unbelievably fine after hours of unrelieved thirst; "rest after toyle, port after stormy seas"— it is the contrast that makes them a foretaste of heaven. Maybe, then, it was the swift transition from the unsavoury streets of Andorra la Vella that made the camp below the Coma Pedrosa seem so paradisal.

We reached the place four hours after leaving Arinsal, where the bus had dumped us. Arinsal stands far up a long side valley west of the longer main *vall* of Andorra, a little old hamlet uglified by a new restaurant and a stream partly filled with old tin cans. It is roadhead, and from it half-a-dozen ravines

like the fingers of an outspread hand run up north and west into
the mountains of the frontier. Northward you can cross into
France over the Port de Bareites; westward—by the longest
and deepest of the ravines—you can climb up into the mountains of Coma Pedrosa and cross the Port Vell into Spain,
which was what we proposed to do. Before starting up the stony
lane that went on from where the road stopped we made a fair
division of the stores we had to carry and lunched sitting on a
wall a little way from the village.

It was good to be out of the oven-like bus in the airier heat of
the afternoon sun, but we had no regrets about using the bus.
The wide motor road to Arinsal had been all uphill and except
for the last mile was bordered by untidy filling-stations and
raw new buildings. Arinsal itself was beyond these eyesores
(apart from a new road that was being blasted out on the
hillside south-west of it) and stood at a gateway of steep
forested hills with the promise of greater mountains beyond.
There was not a soul in sight as we shouldered packs and set
off up the lane.

According to the map, the route to the Port Vell passed a
small lake called the Etang de les Truites, and we had seen
highly-coloured postcards of this lake in the souvenir shops of
Andorra la Vella. The sight of two parked cars where the
motorable lane ended confirmed our suspicion that the Etang
was a goal of the more energetic tourists; but there was still no
one about at the valleyhead where pine-clad mountains rose
suddenly in formidable steepness. Here the lane swerved right,
making a last uphill zigzag from the east bank of the river,
while a footbridge carrying a well-marked path crossed to the
west bank. Arguing from the map, which marked a continuous
path going up the ravine on the west side of the torrent, I led
confidently across the bridge. In ten minutes we were clawing
a dubious way through precipitous thickets with a waterfall
roaring thirty feet below on the right. Jim, who had pressed the
superior advantages of the east bank, had been right—the route
to the Etang de les Truites starts from the top of the lane's last
zigzag and runs up the true left bank of the Rio de Coma
Pedrosa, well above its precipitous ravine. We recrossed the
river and gained a good path waymarked with occasional
splotches of red paint.

It was a delightful path, twisting through steep forest with glimpses of the Pedrosa torrent foaming in its canyons two or three hundred feet below. We met two parties, parents and children, descending the path, a further assurance that we were heading for the Lake of Trouts; and shortly after these encounters found the camp-site we were looking for. The extreme steepness of the rocky slopes had hitherto provided no flat place roomy enough for our three tents, but now the path crept round a semicircular shelf below a miniature cirque of vertical crags. The river fell down the crags in picturesque cascades to carve its way through the rocks of the shelf and plunge into the ravine below, and the shelf was a lovely tangle of flowers and boulders and great clumps of bilberry. It was a puzzling task to site the tents among the rocks, but by 5 o'clock it was done and we were sipping the first and most welcome cuppa and surveying at leisure the lovely spot we had reached. Our shelf was a sort of dress-circle for the theatre of a three-day journey. We looked beyond the descending treetops of the ravine to the narrow Arinsal valley and beyond that to the purple-brown trough of the main Vall where Andorra la Vella (mercifully out of sight) presumably still growled and fumed in its stream of cars. Farther away we discerned—or thought we did—the furrow of the upper Madriu, and above it the less uncertain crest of the eastern frontier stabbing golden peaks into the darkening sky of evening.

Later, Colin cooked a two-soup-packet supper celebratory of our escape from civilisation; and while he cooked Brad collected enough fat and delicious bilberries to provide us all with a satisfying "afters". Counting the ruined barn, this was our seventh camp. The rushing of the torrent was once more in our ears, the smell of woodsmoke once more in our nostrils. I don't find it strange that we, who had been so ill-at-ease in Andorra la Vella, should feel that we were at home again.

At 9 next morning we were sweating out any excess sentimentality on the precipitous path from the shelf to the rim above. The description in my Log has a panting quality: "*Glorious sun. Me stripped to shorts. Very steep climb through splendid craggy scenery. Torrent, cascades. Party going fast. Colin in voice notwithstanding.*" The mercurial man from Llanelli was always happy when there was, as now, a probability that we would be over our pass by lunchtime, and the fact that he could rejoice in song while carrying a pack up a one-in-two slope shows the excellence of his wind. Indeed, we were all in the pink of condition now. There was no suggestion that we should halt by the charming Lake of Trouts, an oval tarn set like an amethyst in a green hollow under the bald slopes leading up to the pass. The path ravelled out in aimless wanderings round the lake and we found no obvious track up the steeps above. Choosing our own routes, we climbed gingerly up an incline of rickety boulders to smaller scree that slid under our boots and arrived, at noon precisely, on the Port Vell, 8,203 feet. Spain stretched away before us in rank on rank of wild mountains to a jagged horizon where sharper peaks sprinkled with snow—the Encantadas, or perhaps their near neighbours the Sabouredo peaks—notched the sky. One last backward glance, clear across Andorra from this western frontier to its eastern one, and then we plunged downward into Catalonia.

It was a very cautious plunge, though. By now we had come to realise that the red-dotted line on our Spanish maps couldn't be trusted. The continuous path marked from the Etang de les Truites across the Port Vell into the upper Barranc de Port Negre simply did not exist. (Incidentally, the crossing took us from one sheet of the map on to another, which showed the same path descending westward not from Port Vell but from a pass called Port Negre.) The very steep slopes directly under the col were trackless and intimidating; I chose a traversing line north-westward on the Spanish side of the crest until a more practicable way of descent showed itself, and even then there was a section where we crawled uncomfortably down on our backsides rather than trust our footing on the crumbling slope. It was a relief to get down into the grassy bottom of a shallow glen, deserted and delightful. We had lunched waterless half-way down the steep descent and paused here for a "five-minuter" and a drink from the stream.

In 1934 my companion and I had tramped up this valley and crossed into Andorra over the Port Vell. In doing the route in reverse I had kept an eye open for scenes and objects that might stir a recollection of that forty-year-old journey, but all was as though I had never crossed the pass before. I could remember, however, that lower down on the Spanish side the river ran through a deep and narrow gorge between vertical cliffs, which forced the only path to steer a precarious and spectacular course round the precipices above, passing through a little cliff-hung village called Tor. There was, I told the others, no hope of a camp-site anywhere on the path above the gorge so we must look for one before we reached it.

Just below our drinking-place we came upon a narrow path following the stream. In ten minutes it had become a wide track, in another twenty a roughly-metalled lane. On either side of track and river the mountainsides rose abruptly but there were small green levels beside the stream where hay had been cut and where three tents would fit nicely. Rounding a steep bend of the track we saw the stone buildings of a *borda* huddled on the hillside and an elderly man and two women walking up the lane towards us. The three debated long and earnestly when I asked them, courteously and in my best bad French, if we might camp on their farm land. At length the man told us we might camp if we paid him 100 pesetas; about £2.30 at that time. We shook our heads sadly and walked on.

Half-a-mile farther down the winding glen was another stone hovel set back from the lane, and a man cutting hay with a sickle in the tiny field before it. He didn't wait to be addressed but hailed us roughly, demanding cigarettes. When I told him we had no cigarettes, which was true, he shouted angrily that it was a lie, that we had plainly come from Andorra where cigarettes were very cheap, and that if we wouldn't give him any we could give him money instead. Again we shook our heads sadly and passed on, this time pursued by what I suspect were terrible curses in the Catalan tongue. There was not much "courtly Spanish grace" about our reception into Spain.

Round the next bend we saw, clinging to the precipices in a fold of the mountainside above us, a tiny and ruinous cluster of stone hovels which could only be the old hamlet of Tor. It was now plain that my path of 1934 had been superseded by the metalled lane we were on; and this was confirmed when we saw below us the perpendicular walls of the river gorge and the lane passing into the gorge on a built-up ledge at the base of the cliffs. We had behind us seven hours of fast, hard going with only brief halts for rest, and when a just-possible camp-site was spotted at the very entrance of the gorge we halted at once. The place proved to be better than it looked at first view. The river foamed and swirled along the base of tall vertical crags on our left and the track squeezed against opposing precipices on the right, but in this one spot there was a few yards of space, occupied by a slightly sloping bank of turf, between track and river. Here we pitched the tents, with due care to see that they sloped so that our feet would point downhill, and proceeded to make ourselves at home.

There never seemed to be much spare time between pitching camp and moving off next morning. Jim had brought a book with him (Herman Melville's *Billy Budd*) and managed to get in some half-hour spells of reading, but for my part I could have done with an extra hour or two at every camp-site to explore its surroundings. With the tents pitched, the next job was to select a suitable place for the fire and construct a fireplace, usually a rather makeshift effort because of the urgency of lighting the fire for that very necessary first cuppa. Firewood at this gorge site was scarce and when all the dry driftwood had been collected from the riverside rocks the thickets beside the lane had to be gleaned for their dry twigs. After the first cuppa there was the unpacking and stowing to be done. All our individual belongings—none of them unimportant —had to be placed along the side of the tent where they wouldn't get lost or rolled on; there was the sleeping-bag to be unrolled, the ground insulation to be inflated, the flies if any slaughtered and swept outside, the food for supper selected and put ready. Colin always rigged a length of nylon line between the pole-tops of two tents, and on this were hung damp socks and any washing; in the gorge stream I washed not only two pairs of socks and a handkerchief but also myself *in toto*, and though the sun vanished behind the cliff-rim at five every item was dry before it did so. The cooking and serving of supper came next, followed by an extra brew of tea and a digestive pipe, and by then twilight was upon us and the need for washing-up and general tidying before it was too dark to see. So it was in half-darkness that I took a stroll down the track when all these household chores had been done.

It was like walking at the bottom of a very elongated lift-shaft, only much more romantic. The black opposing walls of rock, leaning back only a little a hundred feet above, echoed and multiplied the boom of the torrent. Already the strip of luminous green sky overhead between them was speckled with pale stars. Beyond a steep downhill bend of the track the gorge opened a little, to narrow again lower down; here I could look up two thousand feet to the bony crests of mountainsides hardly less steep than the cliffs of the gorge. I could also see movement on the white glimmer of the track below me. Four grey blurs slowly resolved themselves into three cows escorted by a middle-aged Catalan peasant, squat and sturdy. I greeted the man in French and at once he became voluble, having (as he explained more than once) lived in France for several years. The weather? It would stay fine—it was always fine in Catalonia. This road? They'd begun to build it in 1936, to go all the way over into Andorra. The good God knew when they'd finish it. His father had been working on it with others and then they'd all stopped work to go and fight Franco. I asked him if we would pass through any place where we could buy food and other things before reaching Llavorsi (which was more than a day's march away) and his instant enthusiasm was more French than Spanish.

"Alins!" he cried, jabbing a forefinger into my chest. "You will pass through Alins! *Et à Alins vous trouverez TOUT!*"

I thanked him and bade him goodnight, and he stumped on up the track after his ambling cows. When I got back to the tents and reported this encounter, I translated the Catalonian's final words as "At Alins they have EVERYTHING!", and Colin seized upon this dictum as a handy catchword for quotation on many later occasions. But that was after we had actually passed through Alins.

Next morning was cloudless, but so deep was the gorge that we tramped in shadow down its spectacular windings for an hour. After that it was too hot for comfort. The fantastic scenery was a continuous compensation for the dust and sweat. Sometimes we walked between the bare walls of the ravine, sometimes in a more open section where trees and many-hued flowers grew close to the rainbow mists of a waterfall. Once we diverged up a side track to look at an ancient hamlet called Noris that was tucked into the bottom of a gully; two of its primitive houses were occupied, the rest ruinous. The main track, deserted except for our beshorted quartet, kept its steep downhill angle all the way, never more than a few feet from the torrent because there was no room for it elsewhere. It could be called motorable; perhaps by a man who wanted to finish off an old car once for all. But if ever they surface it and take it right over into Andorra it will be one of the most exciting roads in Europe.

This ravine and river, called on the map Riu La Noguera de Tor, is one of dozens of similar clefts in the 100 square miles of riven and contorted mountains between the Andorran frontier and the big southward-running valley of the Noguera Pallaresa, where the main road from Viella to Lerida runs. All the steep-sided ravines, 2,000 feet deep and more, drain southward, and to attempt to travel east-west across such country would be as sensible as trying to walk a strict bee-line from east to west across London. Willy-nilly, we were moving southward away from the main Pyrenean range, with no chance of striking northward again until we reached Llavorsi in the Pallaresa valley. And because in this region the Franco-Spanish frontier turns sharply north for ten miles we would be nearly thirty miles south of it when we arrived in Llavorsi. This circumstance gave an opportunity for one of our projected "raids" into the Spanish mountains. West of the Pallaresa valley is a great tangled massif of peaks and ravines and lakes with the Encantada peaks in the middle and the Cirque de Sabouredo just north of them; by going rather more than twenty miles northward on the Viella road, as far as the high road-pass of the Port de Bonaigua, we could double back southward up a side valley and explore the Cirque de Sabouredo. This plan was agreed to. First, though, we had to do some road-walking to Llavorsi.

Three hours after leaving camp we came to Alins. It was the tiniest of hamlets, standing at the junction of our lane with a wider and definitely motorable road and fast asleep in the hot sunshine of noon. If they did "have everything" at Alins it wasn't on display. But there was a small store that opened at our knocking and sold us bread and tomatoes; and they had beer, which in our state of thirst and heat came near (at the time) to being everything. The party took up its burdens reluctantly for the tramp down the hard highway and made less than an hour's going before halting to lunch in a patch of shade by the river. Morale improved after that. Motorable the road might be, but there was hardly any traffic to harass us, and a little way beyond the lunching-place we found ourselves in another gorge, if anything more spectacular than the one below Tor. However, the overpowering heat dulled appreciation of fine scenery. We felt, and probably looked, like wax candles in an oven. Brad had brought out from the States a large bright-yellow hat with a broad brim (hats are basic backpacking equipment in the Spanish Pyrenees) and I'd noticed that when Brad was tired the brim drooped over his ears. It was drooping now. Plainly an early camp-site was desirable and by half-past three we were scanning the roadside for likely places as we shambled dustily along. For nearly an hour we scanned in vain. The problem was just as it had been twenty-four hours ago—the road and the river took up all the space between the walls of the gorge, and where the gorge widened at a bend the extra width was always occupied by a bank of big rocks overgrown with tangled thickets. At last, about five miles short of Llavorsi, we found a poor site that would have to do. There was a terrace of bare dry gravel in the steep hillside, a dozen feet above the road; probably it had been hewn out by the roadmakers. Here we pitched, uncomfortably. When several pints of tea had been downed we were better able to count the blessings of this site, which included its complete freedom from flies and its delightful coolness when the shadow of the gorge wall fell on it at 6.

In cool shadow, too, we left it next morning. But after an hour we were out of the gorge in hot sun, and on a sweltering tarmac road whose surface was so soft that at every step we indented it with the pattern of our moulded-rubber soles. The valley widened and there were little green fields and a wayside orchard where apples were ripening. As we rounded a last bend a truck belching diesel fumes came hurtling towards us like a mobile outpost of industrialism, and when its dingy smoke had cleared we found ourselves advancing on an enormous electric-power station that filled the valley-mouth at its junction with the Pallaresa. A quarter of a mile away, mistily discerned through a web of overhead wires, was Llavorsi.

The multiplication of power stations and automobiles in once-remote regions is not an unmixed evil. In September 1935 I had written in my diary: "Came to Llavorsi, a dirty little place of hovels and smells." Thirty-nine years later Llavorsi was delightful. With the advent of the hydro-electric works and the big and busy main road it had heaved itself out of the Middle Ages without losing its mediaeval charm but with smells and dirt swept away. The hive of little brown stone-built houses rose up the hill straight from the roadside to the white-washed church that overlooked their clean, flower-hung alleys and steps. In a toy *plaza* twelve paces square we shopped for another three-night expedition.

"They're well supplied here," I commented as Colin and I selected packet-soups and biscuits in the grocer's.

"Ah," said Colin, "but at Alins they have *everything*!"

We had agreed from the outset that if there was a bus along the main road (as there was almost sure to be, for it connected Llavorsi with Viella and the road into France) we would use it to cover the twenty-five miles to the Port de Bonaigua. In Llavorsi they spoke no English and very little French, but we managed to discover that the one daily bus didn't pass through until 3. It was half-past ten now, and arrival on the Port de Bonaigua after 4 meant that we wouldn't be able to reach the Cirque de Sabouredo that night. The solution was Llavorsi's one taxi, whose driver was willing to start at noon and take us up the Bonaigua for 500 pesetas each; 90p. for twenty-five miles was cheaper than fares on British buses and we clinched the deal without hesitation.

In a luxury perhaps slightly alien to the true spirit of back-packing we swirled through the heat of the day up a wide and excellent road—deadly, though, for walking—finishing with an inordinately steep climb by zigzags to the pass, 6,796 feet. The driver shook hands with each of us in turn when he had received his payment, a pleasant custom which reminded me of Norway, and we were left with our packs to survey the Port de Bonaigua.

A bare saddle of turf with the unfenced road running across it and a gaunt stone Customs post, closed and shuttered, beside the road; mild hill-ridges like the Malverns rising on either hand, a view of mountains in the distance to front and rear; two or three cars parked on the turf while their owners picnicked in the sunshine. The Customs post, on this road-pass twenty miles inside Spain, was a reminder that the Port de Bonaigua is a crossing of the logical and physical frontier between Spain and France. For we were standing again on the main Pyrenean ridge; and all the streams in the congeries of valleys to north-ward, where Viella lay hidden in the Vall d'Aran, drained into France. The Bonaigua gap is in the curious "fault" of the High Pyrenees, a formation not badly represented by the conven-tional symbol for forked lightning; the short connecting line stands for the abrupt southward turn of the range where an eight-mile crest links the two west-to-east sections, and our present position was in the middle of this line. Presumably it was some long-ago treaty that straightened the frontier in defiance of its natural line, so that Viella, a Spanish town, stands on the French river Garonne.

At the moment we were more interested in the local topo-graphy. The onward road could be seen coiling like a thread on the mountainsides in its descent to Viella six or seven miles away. Through Viella we would have to pass on our westward way towards the Maladetta, but we were to make a deep southward loop from the direct route—two such loops, as it turned out—before reaching Viella in a week's time. Down on the south flank of the Bonaigua saddle was a wooded valley cutting back into the mountains of the Sabouredo, and a descent into this followed by an uphill march of three or four hours would bring us into the Cirque. We lunched out of sight and sound of the road on a brow overlooking this narrow valley of the Garona de Ruda, and noted its debouchment into the wider valley of the main road north of the Bonaigua. Then, in very hot sun at 2 o'clock, we started down by a little slanting path.

The track up the Ruda glen is motorable for a mile or two, as we could see by a number of cars and tents in the valley bottom below us; a car-owning climber based on Viella could thus drive to within two hours' walk of the Cirque. Our path came down beyond the tents to where the track was an old mule-route paved with big round stones, and we toiled very steeply up it in broiling heat through forests and rocky defiles beside the leaping Garona. Above a barrier of rock down which the Garona flashed in a fine cascade we climbed into a more open *jasse* rimmed with lofty crests. It was half-past four and there were as yet no very striking peaks in sight, for we were still an hour or more short of the Cirque; but here—I confess it with some shame—I threw in the sponge. My case was that of King Wenceslas's Page (if in warmer circumstances) and like him I declared it frankly—I could go no farther. To my surprise the others received this defection rather with relief than abuse, especially Colin, who for once was feeling tired. It must be remembered that our packs laden with three days' supplies weighed a good forty pounds and that we had lately done a lot of load-carrying through the heat of the day when all sensible Spaniards take *siesta*. "Heat exhaustion", more properly body-salt exhaustion through sweating, was probably the cause of our folding-up. At any rate, when a practicable camp-site presented itself a few yards farther on we made camp there. It was a green hollow under silver-grey rocks crowned with sparse pine and juniper, with a meandering brook sparkling through it and the charming white flowers of Grass of Parnassus everywhere. We had met a dozen or more people descending the lower track but here all was peace.

In the morning I had recovered, but Colin was suffering from a splitting headache and an upset stomach. We were away at 8.30 for an upward slog of one hour, at the cool beginning of another brilliant day. It brought us under a rocky rim that hid everything beyond until a last ascent revealed a sight to halt and marvel at. A large and unbelievably blue lake was cradled in grey rock and flower-starred turf. Above it, a jagged frieze against the sky, hung the peaks of Sabouredo.

4. SABOUREDO TO VIELLA

Sabouredo. Arties. Port de Rius (7,686'). Port Vell de Viella (8,182'). Viella. 6 days, 6 camps including 2 nights at the Sabouredo site.

The Cirque de Sabouredo is only one of many such cirques in the region of the Encantadas, and its lake only one of forty or fifty sapphire tarns among the high peaks. Yet again we had to lament the impossibility of spending two or three weeks in this area—and to vow that we would return with more time in hand. To camp, as we did, within a biscuit's toss of the lake, where you can dive from a sun-heated shelf of rock into clear blue water, is the very perfection of camping; or would be if it wasn't for the ubiquitous flies. And in an hour you can be kicking up a ribbon of snow in a shadowed couloir, intent on a 9,000-foot summit.

Of the two days we had in the Sabouredo the first was spent by three of us in comparative idleness. Colin wisely slept off his malady in the tent, completing the cure with a scramble along the lake shore; Brad studied tadpoles and caddis-worms in a neighbouring pond, and I swam briefly in the lake, which is called the Etang de Mig. Jim, however, strode off with his eyes on the summits and after retreating from the final 200 feet of the 9,200-foot Serra de Sabouredo (standard Difficult and exposed) succeeded in getting up the Pic de Ratera, 9,489 feet. From this top he looked into the cirque south of the Sabouredo and had a superb view of the Encantadas peaks. Next day he and Colin set off together to climb the highest of the Sabouredo pinnacles, the Pic de Bassiero, taking with them our thirty feet of perlon clothes-line. A slope of avalanche snow, a couloir of gigantic boulders, and a final clamber on steep rock got them to the summit without using this "rope", though the four Spanish climbers they met there had climbed the peak roped. One of the young Spaniards was a priest and was celebrating Mass for his companions—at 9,631 feet a High Mass indeed. A cup of the wine they were using for Sacrament was offered to the two heretics from Britain; a courteous gesture which went some way towards erasing the unpleasant memory of our welcome into Spain.

While the climbing party was thus amusing itself Brad and I were making a tour of exploration which included three *ports* or cols over 8,000 feet high. The last of these was by way of reconnaissance, for we thought of using it to start a transmontane journey direct to the Port de Rius, on our route for Viella, instead of making the longer and easier circuit northward and back. My Log has a fairly succinct account of this trip—which, to keep in touch with Time, was made on Wednesday August 8th, twelve days out from Ax.

"*We started by gaining the low ridge above the southern shore of the Mig lake. A second and larger lake, startlingly blue, lay beyond the ridge, with the peaks of the Cirque rising sheer from it like the cliffs above the Oeschinensee. Westward up the ridge. More lakes, more fantastic rock spires above. Trumpet gentian (sparse) and lots of yellow arnica just coming into flower at about 8,000. Moving leisurely up granite ledges and bluffs, with many halts to gape at scenery, reached first col at 11—Port de Ratera d'Espot, 8,406, overlooking the Encantadas cirque. View like an Inferno by Doré. Descent on east would bring one down to roadhead at Espot. Several small blue lakes right on the col.*

"After chocolate (Brad) and cigar (me) we traversed broken rocks northward to next col, the Collada Ratera de Colomers, 8,502. Another fine cirque of peaks on the other side of this col, and more lakes. Examined descent on north in case we decide to try this way to Viella, thought it reasonable. But hard pull up from camp and very deep descent. No lunch with us so descended awkward granite bluffs to W. shore of lake and back to camp.

"Off again 2.30 to investigate third and most likely pass, Coll de San Rosa, 8,135. No path from Sabouredo but a reasonable though very steep route up, 1½ hours. On the other side a 4,000-foot drop to bottom of valley, no path, no alternative to a probably hazardous descent through maze of cliff and forest. Returned to camp by another and steeper route diversified by clefts and chasms, alpenrose and arnica flowers."

When climbers and pass-baggers were reunited that evening and a stiff two-packet soup had done its reviving work, the flimsy Spanish maps were spread on a granite slab in the last of daylight. The tentative plan of making directly across country to the Port de Rius was dismissed when Brad and I made our report on the Coll de San Rosa; there was even less enthusiasm for it when we added that we had seen the scar of a new road in the valley below, and counted two cars and six motor-cycles on it. The alternative, if we were to stick doggedly to our objective, was to regain the Bonaigua road and march westward along it to a village called Arties whence the southward loop of our second "raid" could be begun. A topographical note will be useful to explain this.

Viella, the little town that is the capital of the Val d'Aran, stands at the northern foot of a high pass which until modern times was on the most direct route from Central Pyrenean France to Tortosa and the Catalonian seaboard. Travellers crossed the Port de Viella (now Port Vell de Viella, the Old Pass) into the long southward valley of the Ribagorgana between the Maladetta and the cirques and sierras east of it.

Today a road tunnel burrows three miles under the 8,000-foot mountains and the ancient pass is deserted, a *pièce de résistance* for eccentric travellers like ourselves. Our abandonment of the traverse westward from Sabouredo meant that to reach Viella by way of its Port Vell we had first to walk three sides of a square—north, west, and south—before we could turn west over the Port de Rius to the southern foot of the pass.

So we left Sabouredo by that same way wherein we came, regretfully and on a perfect morning. Past our Parnassian camp-site of three nights ago, past the bottom of the slanting descent from the Bonaigua, past the campers and cars in the lower valley and straight on down the motorable lane in increasing heat. "*Meadow and wayside flowers profuse and lovely,*" notes my Log. "*Large pink mallow, 'Welsh Poppy', and a hundred others. Also wild raspberries.*" At noon we lunched, each crouched in his chosen patch of shade under a nettle-based hedge. An hour onward we came to Tredos, a hamlet of mixed architectural styles—Old Pyrenean and Modern Spanish Villa. A brief uphill climb beyond Tredos brought us on to the main road from the Bonaigua Pass and we turned left on it, downhill through the small villages of Salardu and Gessa where garish cafés and bars had recently arrived with the cult of Ski. At 3 a rumble of thunder and a burst of dark rain drove us off the road down a bank where thickets offered some shelter; but Arties, our goal for that day, was in sight half-a-mile away and in a slackening of the rain I led the party at the rate of knots down to the village and straight into a bar. The little place was as dark as a tomb and full of flies, but its beer was cool and drinkable. While the rain outside increased to a downpour, we made out our shopping-list for another three-camp raid and consulted the map (standing under the dripping stone lintel to obtain sufficient light) for that night's camp-site and the way to be followed next day.

This village, a picturesque little township below the Viella-Bonaigua road, is only four miles from Viella where we proposed to arrive in three days' time. It stands at the lower end of the Val d'Arties, up which the map showed a mule-track —but no road—running to the valley-head in a cwm of steep mountains. Here a lesser path was marked striking westward to cross the Port de Rius, 7,686 feet, into the head of the Ribagorgana where the road tunnel has its southern entrance.

At first Colin was for pushing on and camping that night well up the Val d'Arties, but he was overruled three to one. It had been agreed that we would indulge in a square meal when the chance offered; and, as Brad pointed out, the rain and the time of day made a square meal at Arties rather a necessity than an indulgence. But the meal was not easy to come by. There was no inn at Arties (at least my peregrinations in the rain didn't locate one) and only after a deal of inquiring in French, which the folk of Arties doubtfully comprehended, did I locate a place where we could eat. This was a house, a place of pilgrimage it seemed, once occupied by a lady named Palmira Jacquetti, "the Poetess of the Val d'Aran". Having arranged for a meal at 8, we collected our packs and set off in slackening rain to find a site near at hand for the tents. About twenty minutes up the broad track of the Val d'Arties we found a rather dirty spot among the thickets. Like all the other sites we saw or used where other campers had been, this one was fouled with litter; the Spaniards have not yet developed a conscience in this respect. We pitched muddily, sorted out our possessions, and walked down in the twilight to the house of Palmira Jacquetti.

None of us had ever heard of the Poetess of the Val d'Aran and I doubt whether she is much read outside Spain, but we shall remember her by the meal we ate in her house. There are plenty of British and American poets who could benefit from this idea; most of them, I fancy, would prefer that their names should be associated with superb veal cutlets and Cuban sauce, fresh pears, and good wine rather than forgotten altogether. Rice and tomatoes and some other things I've forgotten went with the cutlets and there was a great deal of everything, so that it was replete and singing that we walked back up the lane— by moonlight, for the sky was clearing—and turned in on our muddy site. In the morning the thickets were still dripping wet, but I was up before 6 collecting all the dry wood I could find and at 7 we breakfasted on boiled eggs and tea. Brad liked his egg very soft-boiled. He also tended to be changing a film in his camera at the crucial moment when the yell of "Eggs— come and get 'em!" sounded through the encampment, and so it happened this morning. Brad popped his egg in his jacket

4

pocket while he finished his task, and—the expected happening
—had to spend some time cleaning his jacket in the stream
below the camp. An egg in the shell is worth two in the pocket,
I told him, coining an adage.

Fortunately for Brad's washing, but unfortunately for us, the
sun smote down early out of a cloudless sky and gave us the
hottest morning yet for the trudge up the Val d'Arties. The
track had been widened and was rutted by lorries (I think they
were constructing a new dam in a side-valley higher up) and
two lorries overtook us as we slogged all that morning up a
moderately steep but unyielding gradient. Wild raspberries and
the pointed peaks appearing ahead of us alleviated the toil to
some extent, but it was a relief to come after about three hours
to a junction of upper valleys where the lorry-lane swerved to
the left and our way rose steeply on the right. A lively stream,
the Barranc de Rius, came tumbling down the boulders of a
ravine under the 9,000-foot peaks to northward. The Spanish
map marked a bridge (Pont de Rius) crossing it where the
ancient mule-track left the lane, but the bridge was gone,
obliterated beneath an immense pile of boulders recently fallen
from the peaks. We hopped and teetered from boulder to
boulder and found a very faint track threading its way through
the higher part of the chaos, which took us at length into the
long *jasse* of the glen above. This was a lovely place, emerald
turf, red and grey rock, blue glints from the stream. I recalled
some lines by (of all people) Edgar Wallace:

> *There's some lovely coloured rays,*
> *Pyrotechnical displays,*
> *But you can't expect the burning to admire 'em!*

For it was very hot indeed in the *jasse*. Though we were 6,000
feet up, the cool air usually breathed at that height was absent,
and the gigantic granite boulders reflected the heat on either
hand so that it felt like an August noon on Broadway. However,
it was a granite boulder twenty feet high that provided shade
while we ate a late lunch and dangled our feet in the river; a
taste of heaven after a sip of hell.

Hardly had we started up the glen after lunch when the sky
darkened with dramatic suddenness. Potbellied thunderclouds

rolled across from all sides as black as a tar-barrel. They threatened a devil of a storm and it seemed impossible that the threat could be a vain one. Half-a-mile back we had seen a small stone building, noticed on the map with the word *Baraca*, and after a very short debate we turned and made for it helter-skelter. It was a cube of grimy stone, a prison cell detached from the prison and emptied of everything except some rotting wood; nettles surrounded it and there was nowhere to sit down. We spent a foolish hour in and around this solitary shelter waiting for the storm to break, and when nothing happened except some faintly dyspeptic rumbles behind the peaks we resolved to press on and chance it.

The oppressive heat and the waste of time at the *baraca* combined to make the long climb less than enjoyable. The path was narrow and steep but well-marked, climbing along a ravine with the stream close on the right. It was well after 4 and we were looking out for a camp-site, but there was no flat place in the great rocky trench where we were toiling. The spiky mountain-tops patched with snow that peered over the rim of the trench looked very close above; we could not be far below the pass. Quite suddenly the path curled on to a stony terrace and on our left we saw what looked like the levels and spoil-heaps of a disused mine, with a large wooden shanty not far beyond.

"That'll do us," said Colin. "If there's a bit of roof left we'll sleep there."

There was a bit of roof left, we found, and some broken-down bunks constructed of wire-netting. Moreover, the place had been used as a Refuge within the last ten days or so. It was littered with decaying meat and all manner of filth, and stank horribly. The thunder that still grumbled distantly made the others hesitate about leaving what was almost certainly our last chance of shelter before reaching the pass, but Jove himself with his fist full of thunderbolts couldn't have persuaded me to stay there. A wall of bare rock rose directly behind the shanty, split into cracks and slabs. Up this I scrambled, leaving the rest of the party in debate, and in ten minutes was standing on a narrow crest like Crib Goch with all my ill-humour blown away by a heavenly breeze. I was on the Port de Rius.

From my boots another steep granite wall fell away, but only for sixty or seventy feet. At its bottom was the shore of a big lake, blue even under the overcast evening sky, that filled the whole of the broad saddle of the pass; its farther shore—a good half-mile away—showed between two supporting peaks a low rock-ridge like the one I was on, and distantly beyond that ridge loomed the outlying summits of the Maladetta group. Best of all (for there is nothing so good as playing your hunch and winning) there was a sheltered green nook just below where I was standing, with room enough for our three tents.

The splintered wood that lay about near the shanty gave us our cooking-fire that night and we carried enough over the ridge for next morning. At 7,600 feet we slept warm, and woke to find blue sky opening above. A decision to make a late start so as to reconnoitre the ridge above our eyrie brought the revelation that—once again—we were in a mountaineer's paradise, for from a rock pinnacle east of the camp-site we looked above another and larger lake to a region of peaks and cirques stretching in splendid disarray as far as the eye could see. This is the one frustration a climber, even a climber whose rope hangs in retirement on the study wall, will find in Pyrenean backpacking: he will keep coming to a Promised Land and passing through it. Which after all is only further proof that all journeys are epitomes of life.

The 10.30 start was justified by our camping on the Port de Rius, 7,686 feet, instead of on its eastern side; the Boca Sud (as the southern mouth of the Viella tunnel is called) is at 5,398 feet and we proposed to camp near it, so the day's work involved only about 3½ map miles and not much more than 2,000 feet of descent. In the mountains of North Wales one would reckon on taking an hour and a half over this, given a path. We knew by now that in the Pyrenees it would take us at least twice that time, and in fact the descent occupied four and a half hours including a thirty-minute halt for lunch. A broken mule-track, having contoured delightfully round the north shore of the Etang de Rius—very blue today in its cirque of saw-tooth peaks—plunged down breakneck steeps below the lake's western rim, avoiding what would have been a veritable nose-dive by the skimpiest and most slithery of zigzags. A mile on the map can be an hour of hard going on ground of this kind. From the rim we had had two impressive views: one upward to the snowy Maladetta ten miles away, one downward to the ant-like cars crawling on the road 2,000 feet below. In less than two hours the unstable footing of the zigzags was replaced by a less hazardous path through pines above a torrent (where we halted in welcome shade for lunch) and soon afterwards the path became a new-made forestry road, inches deep in red dust, slanting down into the ample cwm where the Viella tunnel emerges.

It is a curious place, this cwm at the head of the Noguera Riborganza. Splendid mountains cleft by thickly-wooded ravines stand round the flowery pastures where the ancient Hospice of Viella, now half-ruined and serving as a farmhouse, stands at the foot of the old mountain pass. All is as wild and beautiful as any upper *jasse* of the High Pyrenees. Into this wilderness projects a thing like an enormous grey caterpillar, its gaping mouth discharging fumes and occasional automobiles; they have continued the tubular road-tunnel forty yards out from the mountainside, presumably to guard against the blocking of its opening by rockfalls. The road, wide and unfenced, was not busy with traffic but as we came down to it we saw two cars emerge from the tunnel and slither to a halt on the rough grass beside the road. All doors were flung open and the occupants stumbled out clawing at their throats and gasping for breath. There is (we were told later) a ventilation system in the three-mile tunnel; but it doesn't appear to be an efficient one.

We found a good camp-site out of sound and sight of the Boca Sud, on the bank of a stream with pines close behind it, and our cooking-fire was later converted by Brad into a genu-ine backwoodsman's camp fire. It was good to sit smoking and chatting round that fire with the red flames warming one's forepart while the chill night air cooled one's after-structure. Overhead, jutting from a dark robe of forest, the granite peaks towered black against the pale radiance of the rising moon.

Five minutes to eight next morning saw us away to the earliest start yet. At first in the shadow of the peaks, then in increasingly hot sunshine, we toiled up an exceedingly steep and ruinous mule-track, which gave no sign of having been used since last winter at least. This was our sixteenth day of backpacking and the fact that we carried our considerable loads up 2,800 feet in three hours shows how fit we were. Brad, indeed, was in terrific form, leading Jim and Colin at a speed which I preferred not to emulate, following them at an increasing distance until at length they vanished among the gullies and boulders far above. Now ensued a pretty illustration of the hare-and-tortoise fable. I carried the maps; and when I halted to rest I took a look at the Val d'Aran map that showed our present route. The mule-track—now very obscure and at times completely obliterated—was marked climbing north to a dip in the crest of the barrier ridge called the Port Vell de Toro, from which there was no descent on the far side, and thence continuing its ascent due east along the flank of the crest to the higher col of the Port de Viella. When I had toiled up nearly to the skyline straight above I was on the lookout for this eastward turn, and sure enough a path in that direction suddenly appeared skirting the craggy face of the ridge. The rest of the party wasn't in sight and I had the most interesting part of the old pass to myself, a ledge or gallery constructed of huge flat rocks and built round the corners of the crags above a declivity. From a corner halfway along it I paused to look back and down. Half-a-mile away and well below was the broad col of the Port Vell de Toro, and reclining on it—evidently convinced that they had reached the Port de Viella—were my three companions. I hallooed, waved, and pointed onward. But it was some time before they arrived to share the superb view from the true Viella Pass at 8,182 feet.

With time in hand, we lingered half-an-hour there, admiring the snows of the Maladetta across the deep valley whence we had climbed and the vast northward prospect over the Val d'Aran. The first part of the descent was a warning that we hadn't finished with the Port de Viella yet. The path vanished again, lost beneath a crumbling scree of painful steepness down which we crept slowly and cautiously to the grass-grown moraines at the foot. Lunch was overdue when we reached a place for it, but it was an idyllic place. A torrent plashed and bumbled down between flower-crowned boulders at the foot of a bank of bilberry plants. There were a few pines for shade, an essential for comfort down here; up at 8,000 feet the fierce heat of the sun had been tempered by a cool breeze from the

Maladetta snows. A pool below a cascade tempted me and I stripped for a memorable dip. While I was drying out on a hot rock-slab after it nine jet-black butterflies arrived in a crowd and settled on my midriff, making me feel slightly decadent.

In spite of this delightful and prolonged interlude we were pitching the tents at 4 beside a lane in the valley bottom, after a further very hot descent which combined frustration with gluttony. With Viella in sight a thousand feet below, we had borne away to the right from the mule-track, which evidently ran down to join the main road to the Viella tunnel, and found ourselves on a new and muddy forestry road which—as forestry roads are apt to do—began to climb uphill through the pines. Forced to retrace our steps, we came upon fat bilberries in such profusion that we paused to eat our fill; finding, however, room enough for the feast of wild raspberries that awaited us in the overgrown pathway by which we eventually reached the valley.

The camp-site was not ideal but it was adequate. The tents were on a gentle slope of long grass beside the lane—a broad mule-track—that runs down the valley to Viella with the Nere river close on its left; well up on the mountainside across the river was the new main road. We were two miles short of Viella and it was not yet evening, a circumstance that caused Brad (who nursed happy memories of the meal at Arties) to look askance at Colin's selection of soup-packets.

"Why don't we go down and eat in Viella?" he said rebelliously.

Colin and Jim instantly slapped down this suggestion. But I was out of tobacco.

"Remember NATO, *amigos*," I said. "I'll go down to Viella with you, Brad, and we'll do ourselves well."

So the two of us set off down the track. It was not motorable; indeed, it was rocky and steep in places and not at all a route to walk in the dark. Pausing only to exchange creaky French with a gaunt peasant walking up behind two laden horses, we came down to an ancient stone mill by the river, then to newer houses, and then to the busy pavements and swarming cars of a Tourist Centre. It was not quite 6 o'clock when the advance guard of our expedition thus entered Viella.

5. VIELLA TO VENASQUE

Viella. Car to Las Bordas. Port de la Picade (8,200'). Esera valley. Venasque. 3 days, 1 camp, 1 bivouac; then 3 nights in camp at the Esera valley site.

I recalled Viella in 1934: dusty dark alleys, goats wandering in and out of the houses, mules and a daily bus the only traffic. In 1973 it was a Grand Junction of tourism. A white-gloved policeman magnificent of gesture stood in the centre of the *plaza* directing the streams of cars (wisely retreating to the sidewalk when things became difficult) and scores of young Spanish conscripts in uniform mingled with the crowds that paraded past the rows of souvenir shops. And there were hotels. Hotels with terraces where Lagonda-style visitors languidly sipped coffee, hotels with awnings across the pavement, hotels with a string of gourmet-club badges outside. Their menus were on view beside their doorways, and Brad, notebook in hand, scanned each menu in turn as we toured the Viella streets in search of that promised super-dinner. When the tour was complete we had short-listed three hotels whose proffered meals were as super as was compatible with our funds and our slightly outlandish appearance. Licking our lips with anticipatory glee, we made the final choice and marched up the marble steps of a place that would probably have rated three stars with the A.A.

"We wish to dine," said Brad grandly. "A table for two, please."

A raised eyebrow, a shrug. "Your pardon, *señor*, but we do not serve dinner before nine o'clock."

Oh well—the second choice would have to do. And the second choice repulsed us more gruffly.

"No food is served here, *señor*, until nine o'clock."

Then it was the third choice for us. Nothing to eat until nine was the answer there also. It was well after 7 and the early twilight was gathering; we were too hungry to wait ninety minutes for food, and the idea of walking two steep and rough miles in pitch darkness, all uphill, was not to be entertained.

"I'll settle for baked beans or a poached egg on toast," I said. "Let's find a restaurant."

But at the restaurants and the cafés it was the same. Neither for love nor money could food be eaten in Viella before nine o'clock. (I was afterwards told that this preposterous usage prevails throughout northern Spain.) A cowed and miserable retreat began. As we passed the door of a very dimly-lit bar I spotted a row of saucers on the counter. Snacks! We groped our way into an atmosphere of cigarette-smoke and pop music, ordered beer, and grabbed two saucers each from the counter. Five minutes later we were gazing at each other with a wild surmise. Brad's saucers contained, respectively, a mess like a small dog's dinner and a minute section of sausage; mine offered a two-inch square of substance like stressed polystyrene and a tiny, very bony bird. ("*Merle*," said the barman when I asked him; it was a roasted blackbird.) In the end we dined on four rolls and a pint of beer each in this place, and stumbled back up the track sadder and wiser men. However, I had renewed my tobacco supply and Brad carried a bottle of wine, both of which helped to comfort us when we sat listening to Colin's reminiscences of a lordly supper of soup and biscuits and jam.

One other useful thing had been brought back from Viella— the information that the bus from Viella to Las Bordas left at 5 p.m. The loop-raid over the Port Vell de Viella had brought us too far into civilised terrain, and between us and the valley of the Riu de Joeu up which we must go to approach the Maladetta was a nine-mile stretch of busy main road. Las Bordas (or Les Bordas—there are several different spellings for all Pyrenean names) stands just off the main road at the mouth of the Joeu valley where its river joins the Garona. We proposed to camp high up the valley so as to cross the Port de Picade on the following day. For this programme the 5 p.m. bus was much too late, and nine miles of main-road tramping just wasn't on under the broiling Spanish sun. You may ask why we didn't hitch-hike; but who would stop to give a lift to four men with four enormous packs? Even if we separated and hitched for single lifts, Brad was sure to be left—no car-boot would accommodate his huge packframe and Brad and his pack together would fill a truck. No. The answer was a hired car to Las Bordas. And with this in view we were down in Viella by 10 o'clock next morning, Monday August 13th.

4*

The place was as busy as ever. Dodging the souvenir-hunting shoppers, Colin and I bought supplies for two camp-nights plus some extra rations in case a third camp was needed before we reached the next little town, Venasque in the Val d'Esera. A driver was found who would take us to Las Bordas for 100 pesetas (68½p. in 1973) and at fifteen minutes past noon we disembarked in the dusty little *plaza* of the village. The heat was more intense than any we had experienced in Spain and paying 17p. each to avoid three or four hours of road-walking on such a day, we all agreed, was unquestionably the act of four highly intelligent persons.

The motor-road runs on the north bank of the Garona; Las Bordas is huddled in a narrow cwm above the south bank and is reached by a bridge and a steep lane. This has preserved the slightly squalid picturesqueness which characterises the un-spoilt hamlets of Catalonia and saved Las Bordas from the fate of Porté. Three children and a mongrel dog sleeping under the stone drinking-trough were all the inhabitants in sight, but there was a very small shop where Jim and Brad bought big juicy pears. There had been only lump sugar in the Viella shops and I was accustomed to carry granulated sugar in a plastic bottle, so I asked the *señora* of this shop, a handsome woman of sombre mien, if she could fill my bottle with granu-lated. No, she said brusquely; they only sold sugar in kilo packets. Five minutes later, unable to stand the sight of the others munching their pears, I entered the shop again to buy a pear for myself. The *señora* gestured imperiously for my plastic bottle, vanished with it into a back room, and handed it back to me full of sugar. When I wanted to pay for it she would take no money. This small incident quite compensated for our first disappointing encounter with the Catalonians.

Presumably the heat of Hell is a dry heat. Otherwise that afternoon's six-mile slog up the lovely valley could have been a foretaste of Gehenna. But it was a humid heat, different from the scorch of the Spanish sun to which we had become accus-tomed, and I (all skin and bone) actually sweated with the others as we tramped steadily uphill on a newly-metalled road. When at 3 o'clock the sun vanished behind heavy clouds and thunder began its bombardment behind the enclosing moun-tains we hadn't reached the valley-head where we had hoped to camp. But huge drops splashing on the road warned that this was no empty threat, like the one on the Port de Rius, and we looked hurriedly for somewhere to pitch the tents. The road was winding upward through steep woods and nearing the end of its metalled section. Opposite a clearing where road-building material was stacked was a larger clearing apparently used by turning lorries. We rushed one tent partly up a few seconds before the first heavy shower fell and all crowded in for shelter. A slackening of the rain after an hour allowed the other tents to be pitched and I seized the opportunity to collect dry wood; dead branches and twigs hanging clear of the ground are the things to look for in circumstances like these. Two other discoveries were made in that lull: we found that the thickets hid masses of wild strawberries, and that a track below the clearing led to a fine torrent pouring out of a hole in the mountainside higher up. This cascade was the Guells de Joeu.

We were still, of course, north of the main Pyrenean chain, having crossed it at the Port de Bonaigua; we were about to cross it again to the south side by way of the Port de la Picade. The river pouring down the Guells de Joeu—it is the main source of the Garonne—rises on the south side, ducks underground at a place called the Trou de Toro, and emerges 2,000 feet lower down on the north side. This northern emergence was a tremendous sight at twilight, after the deluge that followed the lull in the storm.

My dry kindling had got the fire going and Colin had just pronounced the soup ready when down it came. Supper was eaten under difficulties and in some anxiety. We could hear and feel the surface flood-water surging past the tent, and soon we were out in cagoules digging miniature canals with sticks and pointed rocks. It was a somewhat damp turn-in that night, though the storm passed on at dusk; and next morning, in brilliant sun that set the woodland steaming and sparkling, we set off with wet tents for the valley-head. Half-an-hour's steep walking brought us to it, an impressive cwm, flat-bottomed, with rock-peaks soaring on every side above the last green grasp of the forests. Here in this Pla de l'Artiga there were two new Refuges, youth-hostel style, and one of them was occupied by a party of cheerful Spanish teenagers with the inevitable guitars. (The metalled road came to an end well short of the

Refuges in 1973, but by now there will be cars and caravans and tents in the Pla de l'Artiga.) The new road and the crowd at the Refuge led us to expect that the track up to the Port de la Picade would be populous. The Port is an old and important pass. It crosses the main ridge of the Pyrenees, here the boundary between the provinces of Lerida and Huesca, within half-a-mile of the corner where the ridge becomes once more the Franco-Spanish frontier, so that once you have gained the Picade it is a mere stroll to the start of the descent into France. But not only was the track deserted, it was also hard to find; as with so many other Ports it bore hardly any signs of usage. For us it linked the softer interlude of the Val d'Aran with the grandest part of the Central Pyrenees: the Maladetta and the Posets.

The Picade is an easy pass but long and steep. A narrow and intermittent path crept up the north side of a ravine called the Canal de Pomero, climbing about 3,000 feet in four miles. We stopped for lunch halfway up, close to another *joeu* (the Pyrenean name for a stream that goes underground) which was simply a sizeable waterfall dropping into a large rocky pool that had no visible outlet. The mountainsides were splashed with colour, tall pale-blue iris and the yellow *gentiane* from the root of which the French distil a strongish drink, and the irises were growing at 8,200 feet on the very crest of the pass when we reached it, gasping in thundery heat, at two o'clock. It was the early arrival there, I think, that caused us to ignore the gathering clouds and sit down for a long rest, with magnificent views to look at.

Eastward, looking back above the valley we had climbed out of, the mountains stood clear and sunlit, wave upon wave of jagged crests like a petrified sea. We thought (perhaps erroneously) that we could see the Pic Carlitte, which we had passed sixteen days ago. Westward the peaks of the frontier ridge were ranged on our right hand, their precipices sweeping down into the green Val d'Esera whither we were bound; and at the lower end of the green trough, where it made a sudden bend to southward, stood mountains more exciting than any we had yet seen—Pic Boum, Pic d'Estos, Tuca del Mont, and the lordly Perdighero, 10,700 feet. Across the deep Esera trough, on our left, the huge mass of the Maladetta undulated

in a confusion of rock and snow and glacier. We had barely
time to notice that its slopes were rapidly disappearing behind
a thick veil of rain before there was an ear-splitting explosion of
thunder and we were in the middle of the father-and-mother
of all storms.

Cagoules were dragged on over shorts and shirts but they
were as useless as they would have been in a swimming-bath.
Colossal bucketfuls of water were discharged over us without
pause and with so fierce an impact that the cagoules seemed
likely to be stripped from our backs, and the noise overhead
suggested that Jupiter Pluvius was banging on the empty
buckets. The blue irises were beaten flat. There was no shelter
whatever from the downpour. It would be untrue to say that a
kind of panic seized us; but a strong impulse took hold of me to
get down to the valley in the shortest possible time, and I led
off down the very steep slopes at a headlong pace, short-
circuiting the windings of an immature path. Underfoot, turf
and shale alike were disintegrating into sliding mud. I slipped,
tripped, and turned a complete downhill somersault, pack and
all. Landing fortunately on my feet and unhurt, I pounded on
with Colin close at my heels and the other two not far behind
but invisible beyond a curtain of falling water. I wish I had
timed that descent of 2,500 feet into the upper Esera valley; I
believe it took little more than half-an-hour, and but for the
violent action required was not unlike a parachute descent.
The valley bottom came into sight below through the glass-rod
screen of rain, a grey-green patch littered with huge boulders.
One of the boulders looked rather like a small stone building,
and when we came hurtling down to it, a small stone building
it was.

There were six other drenched creatures sheltering in the
little Refuge: a horse and a mule, a peasant and a peasantess,
and a man and woman who turned out to be British—the first
and only British people we encountered during the whole
26-day journey through the Pyrenees. We exchanged appro-
priate comments on the storm. The Birketts were on their way
down from the Rencluse Hut, having climbed the Pic d'Aneto—
highest summit of the Maladetta—on the previous day, and
had with them a Bleuet stove and dry matches but no tea or
sugar. We had tea and sugar, and a much-needed brew was

got going without delay; the rain had been icy-cold, so that in a space of perhaps ninety minutes we had experienced an almost intolerable heat and a chill so intense that Colin was actually displaying the first symptoms of exposure.

The peasants and their beasts set off into a dwindling rain, the Birketts departed for the valley where they had left their car. We took stock of the situation. The little Refuge, which had recently been rebuilt, had an inner compartment where four men might lie on the straw-covered floor, and an open porch where one could squat in shelter among some dirty stones blackened by previous cooking-fires. We were soaked and bedraggled, it was 5 o'clock, the rain still fell steadily though now much more gently. Decision was unanimous: to bivouac here and find a camp-site farther down the valley next morning. With a justifiable pride in my foresight I produced some dry kindling (gathered below the Port de Rius four days ago) and this with fragments of pinewood scraped from between the blackened stones provided a fire. We were in the middle of supper when a party of nine young Spanish climbers arrived and crowded in to shelter. They were on their way up to the Rencluse Hut, and our agonies of apprehension lest they should elect to stay the night were only banished at 7 when the rain stopped and they all dashed off into the gathering dusk.

In dry sleeping-bags (they had been wrapped in polythene— a sovereign tip) we bedded down in the straw, which was fairly clean and quite comfortable once a dozen or so empty bottles had been removed from it. Waking to the brilliant morning we had confidently expected, our first work was to spread all wet things to dry, some of them on the stone roof of our shelter. An hour or so later we were walking down the most beautiful Pyrenean valley we had yet seen.

The upper valley of the Esera in 1973 was completely wild and unspoilt. Only the faint track that ran past the stone hut was there to show Man's discovery of it. A delightful and way-ward stream wandered through its green levels and pine-clad bluffs—wayward, because it popped underground in places and reappeared a hundred yards away—and all along its length stood magnificent mountains, the forested flank of the Mala-detta under its shining glaciers on the south side, the rock towers of the frontier ridge on the north. Behind us, as we plodded along with our damp socks dangling from the packs, rose the mountain-wall of the Picade down which we had rushed yesterday like the Gadarene swine (and got equally wet), and ahead was an enchanting vista of snow-dusted pinnacles stretching away towards the invisible Pic de Posets, second highest summit of the Pyrenees. At 10 in the morning the valley appeared totally deserted. When we found a perfect camp-site on a wooded shelf above the river it was immediately decided that three of us should spend the rest of that day walking down to Venasque and coming back with supplies for a three-night camp in this idyllic place. Leaving Colin to establish the tents, Jim and Brad and I set off with empty packs for Venasque, at which ancient Pyrenean village (as we had heard) a big new motor-road had recently arrived. The place was 3,000 feet below the upper valley and ten miles from our camp. We had gone less than two of those miles when we saw, with horror, that a newly bulldozed section of the road, curling like a serpent, had reached the very entrance of our unspoilt Eden. Already two or three venturesome motorists had bumped their way as far as the mouth of the wild Remune gorge where the Esera turns south for its plunge down to Venasque.[1]

In the first six miles of the descent by the unmetalled new road we looked into three sheer-sided ravines, as spectacular as a vision of Xanadu, which debouched from the west into the Esera gorge, itself a very fine spectacle if one ignored the road-builders' messes. The third of these, the ravine of the Estos, we proposed to enter in a week's time on the way to our final pass. By the time we passed its entrance, however, we were choking in the thick grey dust kicked up by passing cars on the wide motor-road and were in no shape to appreciate the scenery. Venasque was a haven after this, for its narrow streets and mediaeval buildings stand apart in a loop of the new road and

[1] While I was writing the foregoing pages I received a visit from a friend who had just returned from the Pyrenees, where he had climbed the Maladetta from the Rencluse Hut. He told me that the new road—in August 1975—had come right up the Esera valley, blasting away our "perfect camp-site" to do so, and cars were roaring up and down in front of the little stone Refuge. In 1973 we were told that the new road was to cross the frontier into France, but whether it was to do this by way of a tunnel or by some fantastic route down the precipices on the French side was not known in Venasque.

you are more likely to meet a flock of sheep than a car. The souvenir shops and tourist snack-bars had sprouted here but it was in dark old stores, half underground, that we bought our supplies. The loaf of bread which I carried back up the valley was too hot to touch when I bought it at the door of the bakery and was the size and shape—and nearly the weight—of a Mini car wheel. Darkness had fallen when a very weary trio groped its way through rocks and thickets to the camp-site.

That somewhat purgatorial journey enabled us to explore a small part of a most attractive region. The extraordinary Trou de Toro, where the river vanishes to travel beneath the frontier range as the "Rio Subterraneo a los Guells de Joeu", was reached; Jim made a solo climb to the Epaule of the Maladetta; the Pico de Salvaguardia (9,100 feet) became Brad's first notable Pyrenean ascent; and we all bathed in the sunlit river, did our washing, and decimated the masses of bilberries in the forest above the camp. We saw, distantly, some dozens of walkers and climbers on the path to the Rencluse, but they made little or no impact on the vastness and solitude of the scene. With real regret we watched for the last time the sunset glow fade from the snows of the Perdighero and the flames of an Esera camp-fire grow brighter in the twilight.

Our time was running short. We needed three days for the Grand Finale—the crossing of the Port d'Oo into France— and there were only six days in hand. A two-camp raid was just feasible into "the least known and most absolute part of the barrier between France and Spain", as Belloc called the Posets. On August 18th we shouldered our packs and once again set off downhill for Venasque.

6. THE POSETS

Venasque. Val d'Eriste. Posets. Venasque. 3 days, 2 camps.

Two miles down the main road beyond Venasque is the squalid village of Eriste, additionally uglified by a new power station. From Eriste a side valley, or rather ravine, burrows deep into the mountains to westward, and when you have passed a small concrete dam at its entrance you can climb the old mule-track through most wonderful gorge scenery for half-a-dozen miles and reach an upper *jasse* that might be a thousand miles from power stations and all that they imply. This we did after stocking up at Venasque for two nights. As usual it was phenomenally hot, and as usual we found the ideal camp-site just when it was needed, a woodland glade straight out of a Robin Hood film—though indeed no thousand-foot rock-faces peer down through the leaves of Sherwood.

But the idyll of such places in the Pyrenees is fast fading. The remoteness, forty years ago so real and apparently unchanging, is an illusion. Pastoral Spain, doggedly hugging her ancient way of life and her mediaeval religion, has been an anachronism among the nations of Europe until very recently; but today she has tossed away her mantilla and jumped on the band-wagon with the rest of us, uncaring whether or no the wagon drives downhill to Avernus. "The Spaniards," says James Morris in his book *Spain*, "have for better or worse now plumped for materialism, and you may already see the dams, the new roads and railways, the steel mills and the power plants that are the props of the philosophy." The usual corollaries of that philosophy have been with us in Britain for many years, but they are only just arriving in the Spanish mountains. The mountains must be organised and made productive, and not just for a few shepherds and hardy farmers. They are a barrier to speedy communication so engineers must cut roads and tunnels. Other engineers must harness all available hydro-electric power, and still others must build ski-lifts and cable-car lifts so that the country can tap the same source of wealth as Switzerland and Austria. Mountains have only one valid excuse for existing and that is as a place where industrial workers can have recreation; therefore they must be scheduled as National Parks, officials appointed to patrol them in uniform, and fishing and hunting in them strictly controlled.

This is the Spanish programme, not yet completed but going ahead fast. On the road down to Venasque we saw two uniformed officials catch a middle-aged fisherman as he climbed up to the road from the river. They didn't arrest him, but they did note down his name and address and confiscate his rod and two fine trout. And in the midst of the wildest and most deserted mountain area we visited—at more than 8,000 feet above the sea—we came upon an iron notice, affixed to a boulder, warning us that the hunting here was reserved. This was after we had climbed for three hours across the roughest terrain imaginable.

The wooded head of the valley where we camped was hemmed in by very steep rocky mountainsides. To get within sight, or perhaps reach, of the Pic de Posets was our aim, and to do this we had to climb out over the encircling rim 3,000 feet above. The map marked a path, which certainly started purposefully enough but then lost itself irretrievably in a maze of verticalities split by clefts full of thorny bushes. We tried again, this time seeking a path which led rather wide of our objective but had a dot-and-dash red marking on the map instead of the mere dots of the other. It followed the true right bank of the Eriste stream—a very inexpressive way of putting it, and inaccurate too. For there were two, or it may have been three, tiny cairns to mark the pathless ascent of a rockface several hundred feet high, down (or through) which the river tumbled in a vertical-walled chasm. As scenery it was superb, as a route for walkers it was tricky, and we thanked our stars that there were no 40-pound packs on our backs. To this day I'm not sure that the ravine was crossed where the map marked a crossing, but it was the only place we could find and involved a climb down into the chasm, a hazardous crossing of the torrent, and a climb up the other side. The path, if there was one, failed to show itself in the tilted maze of rocks above, and we sweated upwards—for the morning, as always, was very hot and sunny—choosing our own routes and uniting on a vast rocky hillside with still no view of what lay beyond. It was not far short of noon.

"Too late to try for the Pic de Posets," said Jim with gloomy satisfaction; his efforts to get the party away from camp early had failed.

"You never know," I said. "Keep pushing on."

We pushed on, stripped to the waist in the blaze of heat at 8,000 feet. The angle eased among bare rock slabs and perched boulders (it was here that we found the iron notice-board) and at last we found ourselves on the broad crest. It was in fact the outer edge of a large and curious upper sanctuary a mile or two east of the Pic de Posets. We looked into a shallow valley like a long dish, floored with grey slabs and littered on every hand with boulders large and small. Brad called it "the stone jungle", but it had all the attributes of a desert except flatness, and even on that brilliant day it was hard to see beauty in it. "*Like a moon landscape*," records my Log. "*All around it the savage rock-peaks of the Posets group, grey and red with white snow-streaks. No flowers at all. Grand, gloomy, and peculiar.*" To our left, westward, the stony dish ended in a saddle of boulder-scree and a snowslope, about a mile distant. Above the saddle rose a fine rock-peak, the Diente (Tooth) of Llardana, 10,120 feet, and beyond the Diente a massive russet shoulder mounted skyward, its culmination hidden behind the nearer crests on the far side of the dish.

"That shoulder's the Espaldo de Posets," said Jim, looking up from the map. "Can't be far."

So far as I remember, we heard no more from him until half-past five that evening. The rest of us were lolling in the narrow strips of shade under big boulders, gasping in the heat and wondering whether there was drinkable water in a pond, or corner of a lake, that could be discerned down in the bottom of the dish; when we missed Jim he was well on the way towards the Diente de Llardana, a tiny moving figure in the huge petrified wilderness. No one was anxious to follow him or concerned for his safety. Jim was a climber experienced on British crags and Alpine peaks and could be trusted to return safely from any climb he chose to attempt. Brad and Colin and I decided that a graver and more scientific part of the expedition was ours: we would investigate that gleam of water to ascertain whether or not it was a mirage, and if not we would further experiment to discover whether it would support human life when poured down the gullet.

Big overlapping shelves of rock had masked the reality from us. When these had been passed and the valley bottom was in sight, we saw not only a beautiful little lake shaped like a horseshoe but also several other lakes in a chain above and below it. These tarns, so unexpected and so welcome a sight in that bony place of drought, are called *ibons*, and the dish-shaped valley at 8,300 feet is the Valle de los Ibons. The Valle and the Llano de los Ibons close above it contain no fewer than twenty-one little lakes, many of them with no outlet. In the crags above the north shore of the horseshoe lake (Ibon de la Herradura) there was a narrow couloir with patches of snow in it, and from its foot trickled a stream of ice-cold water. But the Herradura waters were too warm for drinking and muddy too, though the mud only revealed itself when we plunged in—indescribable delight!—and brought it swirling to the surface.

I will not say that our consciences were entirely at ease as we lunched and sunbathed in pleasant idleness on the warm slabs above the lake. The Pic de Posets is (to use Huckleberry Finn's phrase) no slouch of a mountain. It is 11,205 feet high, a rock peak with three glaciers in the cwms between its ridges; we were mountaineers, albeit seniors of the craft, and we had deliberately spurned a chance of climbing it. Our desultory conversation carefully avoided this fact, tending rather to praise the Conservation of Energy as practised by ourselves and to hint that climbing to summits was a waste of time. But the unexpressed feeling that we were not quite the hardy fellows we thought ourselves was there. And since it was now too late to follow Jim—who was almost certainly having a bash at the south ridge of the Posets—we resolved to explore eastward down the chain of *ibons* instead of returning to camp by the way we had come.

It was hardly a nightmare journey, for nightmares rarely have any touch of beauty in them, but it had the fantastic quality of a dream—a post-lobster dream, perhaps. Down lopsided corridors of riven rock we clambered from pool to pool; sometimes peering into the chasms by which little rivers, miniature Alphs, foamed and rumbled from one *ibon* to the next, sometimes checking direction with the compass in an *ibon*-less box of stone where the only view was of the sky overhead. I confess to being vain of my route-finding skill, and I swaggered a bit when we duly reached a large *ibon* past which, the map asserted, there was a major path which eventually descended steeply into the upper Eriste valley. And here indeed *was* a stony way between the crags, which could be an ancient mule-track running south on the west side of the lake. In five minutes it had vanished and we were clambering down boulders and jumping dicily across the tops of waterfalls. Then it reappeared as a shelf overhanging a ravine; disappeared beneath a huge rock-fall; turned up again as a ledge on the brink of the 200-foot drop to the gorge of the Eriste; and there vanished completely. It had to be found. The precipice was by no means sheer, for its successive "boiler-plates" of grey rock were not long and were separated by ledges. But the rocks were steep and the ledges invariably crammed with tall and thorny vegetation, and because the angle steepened lower down it was impossible to see more than a hundred feet of the route below. I probed gingerly downwards and once more located the path— two zigzags of what had once been a mule-track but was now an overgrown ramp of rubble and maquis. When it plunged downwards into an impenetrable tangle of thorns we traversed leftward across slabs and lost it for good.

"This is nonsense," declared Colin. "Straight down—you can't fall far."

He lowered himself down a steep slab, below which no feasible route was visible. Brad and I left him to it and sought a way that had at least a more hopeful start.

According to Sir Walter Scott, "a mixture of danger gives dignity to the traveller"; but there was very little dignity about our subsequent progress as we slithered down rock as rough as gabbro and later swung from treetrunk to treetrunk—a pair of clumsy Tarzans—through a tangle of pine-trees that had contrived to root themselves in a near-vertical precipice. A mildly hazardous crossing of the torrent in the gorge-bottom seemed quite pleasurable after this. Twenty minutes later we limped into camp, to find that Colin was not (as I had half-feared) lying on some inaccessible ledge with a broken leg but was back before us and nearly ready with a brew of tea. We were still steadily drinking it when Jim strolled in, looking nonchalant, to inform us offhandedly that he had climbed the Pic de Posets.

He had gained the Espaldo or south ridge of the peak without much trouble though the route-finding needed care. The ridge rose straight to the narrow rock crest ending in the summit—"nothing anywhere much harder than Crib Goch"— where he had made no halt but started at once to descend; the gathering thunderclouds and the electric tension in the atmosphere made an 11,000-foot summit a place to get down from as quickly as possible. Using a slanting fault on the east face, Jim reached the snow of the Glacier de Posets and having crossed it traversed the stone jungle and came down into the river glen. It all sounded simple and easy, the way he told it, but it was a notable feat of mountaineering and we congratulated him accordingly. The thunderclouds which had sent him racing down from the summit were still hanging about overhead that evening, but all they produced down at our sheltered camp-site was a fifteen-minute shower; though the fact that the river a few yards from the tents rose a foot or more in the next hour showed that there had been much heavier rain higher up.

Next morning the Posets expedition withdrew in good order by the way it had come. The cloudless sky promised a hot day, but by striking camp early and getting on the march at 8 we were able to go all the way down the Eriste gorge in cool shadow and at top speed. There followed the hot and dusty two miles of main road up to Venasque (reached at 10.30) where we stocked up for the last time and drank a good deal of coffee and beer. There would be no more southward "raids", the westward journeying was done. Our way now was to the north.

A few pages back I was writing that the remoteness of the Pyrenees is today an illusion. In the Posets, as the reader will have noticed, the illusion is well sustained. The one full day we spent in the neighbourhood of the main peak was Sunday August 18th, the very core and climax of the summer vacation when in Britain you have to wait your turn in the queue to stand on the summit-cairn of Snowdon. We covered a considerable amount of ground that day, from the Eriste valley to the Valle de los Ibons, and the only living creatures we saw were nine very large birds (not eagles, of course; lammergeier, perhaps?) circling slowly high overhead. Jim climbed to the second highest summit of the Pyrenees and had the whole mountain to himself. The paths marked so boldly on the Spanish map of the Posets were either non-existent or disused and impossible to follow, and there was not a single empty Coca-Cola tin anywhere. It was a region we would have been sorry to miss seeing if only for its startling contrasts—the Eriste gorge all "bowers of greenery for poets made", the Valle de los Ibons as bare and lonely as Shelley's desert where the statue of Ozymandias lay broken. It was so in 1973, but by 1976 even the illusion of remoteness may have gone from the Posets. It would be worth any backpacker's while to go and see.

7. VENASQUE TO LUCHON

Venasque. Val d'Estos. Port d'Oo (9,655'). St Aventin. Luchon.
3 days, 3 camps.

On Monday August 20th we were at Venasque in Spain, eight miles south of the highest and most rugged section of the main Pyrenean crest. On Thursday August 23rd we had to catch the northbound train from Bagnères de Luchon, a day's march north of the crest. No road pass crosses this 25-mile stretch of the range, and if we failed to get over the Port d'Oo, which was likely to be the most difficult as well as the highest of our passes, we would certainly miss the train with its prearranged luxuries of booked seats and couchettes to Paris. So although we dallied for well over an hour in Venasque after the long hot walk from the Eriste valley camp there was an air of urgency and resolve about the party when it left the little town fifteen minutes after noon. Once more, but for the last time, the packs were at their heaviest, with food for three days in them. The fierce Spanish sun (it was to be just as fierce in France, though) smote on our backs as we trudged up the dusty motor-road which three of us were treading for the fourth time. However, this time there was only a two-mile stint to be done along the road, as far as the Bridge of Cuberre.

In 1934 Basil Gethin and I had crossed this ancient bridge (said to be eight hundred years old) and gained the mule-track, as it was then, leading down to Venasque; we were lucky to have got safely over the Port d'Oo from France, having encountered nine successive thunderstorms on the way. Then the Bridge of Cuberre had been the only crossing of the Esera river for the laden mules which were the only traffic. Now the motor-road crossed the river by a hideous concrete bridge higher up, and the old bridge—still a thing of beauty—was fast decaying and had lost one of its walls. By it we crossed to a zig-zag path climbing into the jaws of a narrow and sheer-sided ravine, after lunching and incidentally lightening our burdens by the weight of four delicious peaches bought in Venasque.

The lower Estos ravine hadn't escaped the eye of the hydro-electric engineer, or the subsequent mess of pipes and rubble and dams. But once this had been left behind the scenery was as

wild and splendid as we could have wished for in our last
Spanish valley. The track, a good one, contoured low down on
the flank of the ravine and ascended more gently than the path
up the Eriste, opening new vistas of crag and torrent at every
turn. It crossed to the right (west) bank of the river and by a
short climb of steeper angle gained the long upper *jasse* below
the impressive peaks of the frontier range on our right, chief
among them the Perdighero, 10,560 feet, whose snowy pedestal
loomed behind the sharp rock pinnacle of the Tuca Gargallosa.
The well-trodden track showed that the Estos valley was
frequented by walkers and climbers; indeed, we knew this
beforehand, having somewhere come across a tourist leaflet
that sang the praises of a new-built restaurant that had replaced
the old Cabane de Turmo two miles below the Refugio de
Estos, which is the climbers' hut whence the Perdighero, the
Posets, and other peaks are climbed. It was no surprise, therefore, to overtake two parties of half-a-dozen young Spaniards,
youths and girls. They put on a spurt and passed our steadily
plodding caravan; and twenty minutes later we passed them
lying in attitudes of exhaustion halfway up a steepening of the
path. They were carrying only small rucksacks or Airways
satchels, and it was highly satisfactory to four older persons
carrying heavy packs to demonstrate the physical superiority of
age over youth. It was satisfactory, too, to find that the Cabane
de Turmo was still an old shell of Pyrenean stone half buried in
long grass and nettles. The Spaniards have this habit of
anticipating progress in their tourist literature and the splendid
new restaurant was still a twinkle in its planner's eye. Near the
Cabane we recrossed the river to a cairned path that followed
its left bank towards the Refugio de Estos, leaving the main
track which goes to the head of the valley and crosses the
Puerto de Gistain into the wild country west of the Posets—an
attractive route which we would have liked to follow.

But now the mountainsides on the right were opening in a
huge rocky slope with snow-powdered peaks peering over its
upper rim. Somewhere up there was our pass for tomorrow.
Even those lower slopes of ledge and rock-wall looked tricky and
there was no obvious route that Brad and I could see as we
stared up at them. As we stared we noticed that the sky had
suddenly darkened, and turned to scurry along the river bank

to where Jim and Colin were already unpacking their tents. We had the camp pitched in the nick of time. Down came the rain as we bundled inside the tents. It was a rainstorm comparable to the one we had experienced on the Port de la Picade, and for an hour it beat deafeningly on the tent fabric while we squatted in shelter with the smug satisfaction of old Pyrenean hands; until we realised that there wouldn't be a scrap of dry wood anywhere for the cooking of supper.

There's no smoke without flame, so I still maintain that my cooking-fire was alight twenty minutes after the rain ceased. Brad thought otherwise. Employing a ruse of Davy Crockett (or it may have been the Deerslayer) Brad had borrowed a candle-end and with it had produced a cheering blaze from some steaming pine-twigs, and I was not too proud to accept a flaming brand for the stimulation of my own fire. The customary cuppa of course came first, greatly delayed by the downpour, and after it the customary soup. It tasted very good as it always did. But after 22 soup suppers in 24 days it was natural enough that the minds of some of us should thrust forward to Luchon and the meal we planned to have there. It was to celebrate Brad's birthday, which happily coincided with the day on which we hoped to arrive among the myriad eating-houses of Bagnères de Luchon, and as we sat smoking round the red embers in the darkness of 9 p.m. we resolved that it should be something really good.

"Roast blackbird, maybe?" suggested Colin; and was very properly ignored.

"Blueberry pie," sighed Brad longingly.

"A bottle of decent wine, anyway," I said.

Jim got to his feet. "First cross your pass," he said. "I'm turning in."

The Port d'Oo merited an early start but the wetness of tents and gear delayed us. Nothing, naturally, had dried out during the night and to start a difficult 4,000-foot ascent carrying a lot of extra weight—for wet tents are much heavier than dry ones—would have been foolish, so we boosted up the morning fire and spread the steaming tents before it until the sun appeared at his eastern gate and set the whole camp-site steaming as well. It was nearly 9 when we started for the pass, striking directly up the mountainside, due north. Less than half-a-mile away to our left the stone-built Refugio de Estos stood on a rocky slope beyond a wide gully with a stream running down it, and we expected to join higher up a path which our map marked as starting from the Refuge and continuing over the pass. In fact, there is no path over the Port d'Oo and the first path we struck that day was fifteen hundred feet down on the French side.

The slope we were climbing had no resemblance to a valley but the Spanish 1:25000 map calls it the Valle de Gias. From that map, which shows contour lines twenty metres apart, you'd think the Valle de Gias was an even slope of grass or possibly scree, for not one crag or ravine is indicated. It was all crags and ravines, set at inordinately high angles and jutting successive battlements of rock a hundred feet overhead so that it was impossible to plan your route for more than that distance. Tiny cairns spaced at very long intervals did little more than marshal us the way that we were going, and did that rarely; for it takes a sharp eye to discern two little rocks, one on top of the other, in the midst of a tilted chaos of rocks. They were welcome, however, as assurances that there was a practicable way through the obstacles ahead, and the cry of "Another cairn—over to the left!" was encouraging to the momentarily bewildered route-finder. The route climbed steadily over boulders and up slabs that were hot to the touch. There was a cooler and mildly exciting section where a cairn challengingly invited us to traverse an exiguous ledge on the shadowed wall of a ravine, with the torrent leaping hungrily just below. The emergence from this was into a curious maze of stony alleys between great masses of piled boulders, where we looked in vain for a small lake shown on the map.

The stony maze was reached after two hours' going from the valley. It was not so steep as the lower slope and gave a first view of the frontier peaks peering over its farther rim, romantically jagged and banded with snow. The rim looked impossible of access, so steep were the walls below it, and we had halted to discuss the advisability of making for a nose or buttress a couple of hundred feet high that seemed to offer a rock-climber's route—there were no cairns hereabouts—when we caught sight of two tiny specks moving on the crest of the buttress. It was a timely indication. The nose, when we reached it, was as steep as it had looked; but as so often happens with granite there were ledges and clefts thatched with turf which provided an airy scramble not unduly hazardous for the heavy-laden. The two we had seen from afar were resting above the buttress and we chatted with them in a clumsy mixture of French and English. They were young Spanish climbers from Barcelona, and their plan was to cross the Port d'Oo, traverse eastward on the French flank, and return over the lower Portillon to the Refugio de Estos. They appeared to know their way about in this area. We should have known better than to trust in "those awful Goddesses, Appearances".

All the three hours of this steep and tortuous ascent I was trying to recapture some familiarity with it. Down from the pass to the Valle de Estos I had certainly come in 1934, and I couldn't recognise any of the landmarks or remember any of the mild hazards. Perhaps such chances of mountain travel are less momentous when one is 26. But I was more than ever convinced that my companion and I were exceedingly lucky to get safely down the way we were now going up.

There was another circumstance on this ascent to the Port d'Oo, which I mention for the warning and comfort of other senior backpackers. Log quote: "*At 8,000-plus began to breathe badly. Lay down. Brad stayed with me, Jim and Colin had disappeared ahead. Went on, slight heart pain, halting repeatedly. Came up with the others resting just below final rock-wall of pass. No further trouble after rest and food.*"

The Port d'Oo (*Puerto de Ôo* on the Spanish maps) is, as Belloc says, little more than a depression in the very high frontier ridge; but it is a longish depression, a crest or narrow wall spanning the interval between the Pic d'Oo and a nameless peak half-a-mile east of it, both peaks being less than 200 metres higher than the pass itself. It has a characteristic typical of Pyrenean passes and important to anyone following this route: the seemingly obvious crossing-place of the col is not the point where you should cross it. Approaching from the south, as we did, you toil up a long and steep slope of boulders and large stones towards the centre of the 50-foot rock-wall on the skyline of the pass. At the left-hand (west) end of this wall, where it merges with the ascending crags of the Pic d'Oo, you see a rather higher mass of unpleasant-looking scree. This is the true pass, and from the northern side it can be seen quite clearly to be the only reasonable way over. We took the wrong way by imitating the Spaniards in front of us.

The two lads from Barcelona had forged ahead up the boulder-slope and as we followed we saw them climb straight up the 50-foot rock-wall. After a brief lunch at the foot of the wall we climbed it by the same route. It was extremely steep but easy—large holds, a step or two demanding care in balancing a heavy pack, and a simple swing up on to the crest. We were on something closely resembling Crib Goch in North Wales, but with the deep valleys of France 4,000 feet below in front and the wild ranges of Spain stretching far away behind us. Nearer at hand on the French side, dark precipices and snowslopes heeled over above the wildest and gloomiest of mountain lakes—

Still waters between walls
Of shadowy granite in a gleaming pass

—sunk in a basin of snow and rock a thousand feet beneath our boots. Its black surface was half covered with flat pieces of ice, large and small, like a jigsaw puzzle ready for a giant to assemble. Between us and it was a boulder scree ending in a downward alley of snow. The boulder scree was not only far steeper than the one we had climbed to reach the pass but also obviously dangerous, as was shown by the pale scars of recent rock-falls and the many impending blocks poised ready for a tumble. There could be no way down that crumbling wall, we agreed. And then we spotted the two Spanish climbers.

They were a long way down the boulder scree and some distance from each other, halted as if in perplexity. An instant after we caught sight of them they were enveloped in a dense cloud of grey-brown dust shot through with yellow sparks, and a moment later came the enormous rending crash of the rock-fall they had dislodged. It was a second or two before the dust-cloud thinned and—to our great relief—we saw both Spaniards again, crouched and clinging to the rocks. They were unhurt, for they presently began to move very cautiously away to the right and were soon hidden by the intervening boulders.

We could now consider our own case. We could go east along the crest, but that would only land us on a snowslope

angled like a sheet on a clothes-line, an impossible descent
without ice-axes. The ridge to westward rose in tottering
pinnacles and knife-edges where a rope would be essential.
There was only one way that gave a chance of safe passage:
with care, we could get down to a sort of promontory formed
of immense boulders, rocks so big that our added weight on
them could hardly send them down. From here we would have
to launch out on a descending traverse of the boulder-slope
heading for the upper end of a brief snowslope. This western
half of the boulder scree looked slightly less steep than the
place where the Spaniards had been seen, but it was deeply
cut into by a sheer-walled ravine on whose upper rim the loose
scree hung poised. We had to traverse above that upper rim.

The first part, down to the big rocks and between them, was
easy and felt safe. But out on the roof-like slant of smaller
rocks things were not so good. You could tread as delicately as
Agag, but every rock shifted slightly downwards underfoot;
and always when you looked down beyond your right knee
you saw the gaping red-walled chasm. I was more worried
about Brad than about myself, for he had less experience on
such places and was placing an extra five or six stone on the
footing that moved beneath my light weight. However, we all
got across without incident and went skipping and glissading
down the snow in the exhilaration that always follows such
periods of tension.

The snowslope was an arm of the little Glacier d'Oo, which
is not crevassed and was (I think) much shrunken since 1934.
My memory of that former crossing seemed to return to me
here, and I felt sure we had then come up round the east shore
of the Lac Glacé, as the ice-floe lake is called. A reconnaissance
down the snow to its steepening above the lake showed that
either my memory was at fault or the terrain had changed in
four decades; the east shore was all sheer bluffs and snow-filled
couloirs, totally impassable. It was necessary to traverse
difficult ground high above the west shore before we reached a
line of descending humps, the last of which overlooked the upper
jasse of the long Vallée d'Oo. The Lac Glacé is borne in a sort of
pigeon-hole of the mountains, and from the outer edge of this
a declivity drops very steeply to the green bottom of the *jasse*,
where we could descry a plain path. It was not clear how we

were to get down to the path but there was no doubt that we should do so. And I for one felt more than a little sad. Our last Pyrenean pass was behind us, the uncertainties and triumphs of route-finding at an end. That path, in a few miles, would end on a motor-road; the road would end at Luchon and the train home. This was a place of long farewell to all that greatness in the southern sky.

We paused to look back at the splendid frontier peaks, black precipices and white snow. We saw, now, the route by which we ought to have crossed the pass. And we saw the murky thunderclouds come swooping over the Port d'Oo and blot it out of sight.

"A cairn!" called Jim from lower down where he was huddling on his cagoule. "Down there on the edge."

It marked the start of a little breakneck path that zigzagged down into the valley. The thunder crashed as we clawed and scrambled down it. The rain stormed down as we tramped singing along a stone-paved path to the Saussat lake, passing three drenched French walkers on the way. Close to the Lac d'Espingo, which is just round the corner from Saussat, there is now a big new climbing-hut, well filled with young French men and girls. We got in out of the rain and bought beer ("I perceived by the price that it was dissolved jewellery, and I perceived by the taste that dissolved jewellery is not good to drink") and in view of the weather inquired the cost of sleeping-quarters, which was in line with the cost of the beer. Twenty minutes after leaving the Refuge d'Espingo we were making our penultimate camp on the least comfortable of sites in the most romantic of positions.

Below the Refuge the track, broad but steep, doubled round below a lofty bluff to a heathery edge directly above the precipices falling to the beautiful Lac d'Oo. The rain had stopped and the evening sky was clearing. There was no flat site anywhere on the slopes that plunged a thousand feet to the blue-green lake waters in their cirque of heights, but on the left of the path a little dome of grey rock, with a grassy shelf round it, capped a buttress overhanging the drop to the lake. We pitched the tents with difficulty but got a fire going with ease, for the heavy rain hadn't reached this far down and there was old juniper wood and heather roots among the rocks. A magnificent waterfall fell down the vertical cliffs into the Lac d'Oo, but it was a foot-wide stream nearer at hand that provided us with water; not without hazard on our part. I remember straddling the stream on slippery footholds to brush my teeth, and glancing downward between my legs to the black waters of the lake a long way below. Another memory is clearer and more colourful. To quote my Pyrenean Log for the last time: *"Shan't forget last scene of this evening. Huge dark peaks looming in background, pitch-black depths below, red flames of our fire dancing on the rock dome. Flames cast shifting light on intent faces of Jim and Brad holding out their wet socks to dry on bits of stick."*

This was the real end of our mountain journey. There was to be one more full day of lane and road walking, one more camp—in a wayside field at St Aventin—before the celebratory dinner in Luchon and the home-bound train at 8.20 p.m. But the Lac d'Oo, to which motorists may walk from their parked cars and find a good restaurant by the lake shore, marked for us the exit from the Pyrenees. Little more than twenty-four hours after leaving it we were in crowded Luchon and Colin was looking all round him at the splendid avenues, the lovely gardens, the multitudes of shops and cafés, the general display of opulent abundance. He turned to me.

"But at Alins," said Colin, "they have *everything*!"

He was grinning; but I swear a nostalgic tear glittered in his eye.

THREE

The Pennine Alps

1. MARTIGNY TO AROLLA

Martigny. Verbier. Col de Louvie (9,640'). Col de Prafleuri (9,844'). Lac des Dix. Col de Riedmatten (9,567'). 3 days, 3 camps, plus 1 day and 1 camp weatherbound.

The two tents, Itisa and Good Companions, had been pitched on the shelf of mountainside at 4 in the afternoon of July 20th. At nightfall of July 21st they were still there. In the Good Companions Colin Morgan and Alex Blair argued about Grand Opera. In the Itisa Jim Thomas was reading Patrides' book on Milton's epic poetry while I strove to swallow two of the six king-size antibiotic tablets that were supposed to be curing me of influenza. Outside the rain dripped on out of the dense and freezing cloud that hung across the Val de Bagnes from the Grand Combin to the invisible Pic Mont Fort above our heads. It wasn't an auspicious start to the end-to-end traverse of the Pennine Alps by paths and passes we proposed to do.

It was perishing cold up here at over 8,000 feet, but it had been very hot on the 20th for the 3,500-foot climb from Verbier to this stony cwm below the Cabane de Mont Fort. At Martigny, where the train from Paris had discharged us at 8 a.m., they had told us that this was the first fine day in the Valais Alps for a fortnight; it looked like being a flash-in-the-pan. The brief and scenic train trip from Martigny up to Le Chable and a quick change to the waiting bus had brought us in an hour to Verbier, an up-and-coming ski resort at 4,600 feet where we had stocked up in some very sophisticated shops for a three-camp journey to Arolla. Then our untried load-carrying muscles had been tested on a very steep climb, by a waymarked track through forest to bare mountainside on the Mont Fort path in sweltering heat. If hearty sweating hastens the departure of 'flu then I was well on the way to recovery by the time I

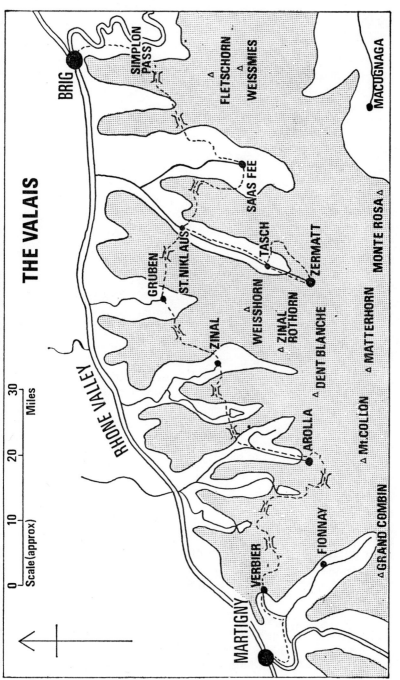

THE VALAIS

RHONE VALLEY

Scale (approx)

0   10   20   30

Miles

MARTIGNY

BRIG

SIMPLON PASS

FLETSCHORN

WEISSMIES

MACUGNAGA

SAAS FEE

GRUBEN

ST. NIKLAUS

TASCH

ZERMATT

ZINAL

WEISSHORN

ZINAL ROTHORN

DENT BLANCHE

MONTE ROSA

MATTERHORN

AROLLA

Mt. COLLON

VERBIER

FIONNAY

GRAND COMBIN

5

dragged myself to the broad hanging shelf of turf and rocks where the others were pitching the tents.

The path leading to the Cabane, a C.A.S. hut, is easy to follow. The hut (we were to pass just below it on the 22nd) is a two-storey stone building splendidly situated for views and for ascents of the 11,000-foot peaks at this eastern end of the Valais mountains. We planned to branch southward on a lesser path which contours the knees of the said peaks to a point north-by-west of Fionnay, in the valley 5,000 feet below, where a break in the chain of peaks allows it to double back northward and cross the chain by the high Col de Louvie. Too hopefully as it turned out, we planned to cross the Grand Desert glacier on the same day and get over the even higher Col de Prafleuri down to the Val des Dix. The start of this lesser path was obscure on the map and more obscure on the terrain when we came to look for it. Before the cold cloud hid everything an hour after pitching camp two possibilities had been discerned on the extremely steep and broken mountain-face south of the tents: a track slightly lower than the camp, and a threadlike line ascending higher up across screes and buttresses until it vanished among vertical crags. Obviously we had to have clear weather to help us on the initial section of the journey. Hence the day's delay when the blanket of cloud failed to lift.

I was the only one of us who was glad of the delay. Lying in my sleeping-bag guzzling antibiotics, I was able to rid myself of most of the post-'flu weakness; a couple of strenuous days were to clear away the rest. The others, more impatient, made a sally or two into the mist, and Alex set forth in the drizzle for a solitary ascent of a craggy summit north of the tents. Alex Blair was the baby of the party (we reckoned he wouldn't see 35 again) but its most skilled exponent of climbing on rock and snow. The quartet that had backpacked through the Pyrenees the previous year was short of Brad Herzog, constrained by his profession to stay in Massachusetts taking photographs of Harvard University from rooftops and helicopters, and Alex was a welcome stand-in. He was a quiet and reflective type, the imperturbable Englishman *par excellence*, and on at least two occasions his prompt perception and ready lead were to get us down a tricky place that had given the rest of us pause. He had modified his Good Companions Major tent, less roomy than the Itisa Senior, to make extra space for packframes and food and stove-cooking in the tent. Each tent-pair did their own cooking on Bleuet S200 stoves burning Camping Gaz, a handier arrangement than carrying the larger stove and utensils that would have been necessary for four; we could not rely on wood fires as we had done in the Pyrenees, where the treeline is higher than in the Alps, and since we were to arrive in Swiss tourist centres every three or four days we could count on obtaining replacement Gaz cartridges. A cartridge gave about two-and-a-half days' cooking and tea-brewing for two, so a spare for each stove was always carried.

The end-to-end traverse of the Valais Alps had been mainly Colin's idea, a parallel to our 1972 Oberland journey on the other side of the Rhone Valley. It presented a route-finding problem different from that of the Oberland or the Pyrenees. The chain of the Pennines, culminating in the Matterhorn and Monte Rosa, runs west-to-east as the Swiss-Italian frontier, with long branch ridges striking northward from it. Between these ridges, which are very high near the frontier, deep valleys reach down to the Rhone valley, all running due north. Our west-east traverse had to leapfrog in and out of the valleys and we wanted to cross their containing ridges as near the big peaks as possible; but the passes that link Arolla and Zermatt and Saas more or less directly are difficult glacier passes demanding axe and rope, so to visit these three centres (which was our intention) it was necessary to cross the "walking" passes of 9,000 feet or so over the ridges farther north and double south up the valleys and back. Starting from Martigny and finishing at Brig, we reckoned we could do the journey in three weeks and have the occasional off-day on the way. So it proved. And of the three journeys this one was to be the most exacting in mountaincraft.

As usual, I kept a scribbled "Log" of our travels, sometimes written up by candle-light in the tent, sometimes at the lunch-time halt. These jottings are terse but record spontaneous reactions on the spot, so I propose to quote from them occasionally as before, beginning with an entry on the second morning at our first camp: "*A SUPERB morning! The Combin and Mont Blanc groups glittering in the west—spirits of party zoomed up in spite of very cold night. We are away at last.*"

It had indeed been a cold night. Ice dropping on our noses from the tent roofs woke us to the realisation of the warming sun. Outside, everyone exploded in enthusiastic yells. After the prolonged gloom the sight of those shining snows rising beyond the shadowed Val de Bagnes into a clear blue sky was the best of tonics. Looking the other way, we saw the huge and craggy corrie in whose lap we had been lying for forty hours, a corrie whose upper walls were capped with snow and whitened lower down with last night's fall. Outward across the southern wall ran a barely-discernible white line, crossing steep couloirs to a corner buttress that overhung the Val de Bagnes. This upper path, now that we could see it in relation to the other features, was undoubtedly the start of our route. Breakfast was a frugal one, for Arolla had now to be reached on two days' rations and we were beginning to doubt whether the Louvie and Prafleuri passes could after all be crossed without camping between them. We were away at 8.30.

Regaining the path that led upwards to the Cabane, we followed it for ten or fifteen minutes until a not very obvious branch path turned off to the right, rounding the head-slopes of the corrie to the screes below the southern wall and crossing them to connect with the thread-like track we had seen. Locally this tenuous trail is called the Promenade des Chamois. An apt name, I thought as I balanced my thirty-five-pound pack round its exposed corners and across slithery couloirs. The growing heat of the sun had melted the snow-powder and turned the shale of the couloirs to mud; since every gully ended thirty feet down on the rim of a precipice, the skidding of one's vibram soles on their surfaces was not at all funny. Down one of them hung a chain, by which you hauled yourself up hand-over-hand while dislodged gobs of mud showered over the edge below into space.

"You have nothing to lose but your chain," quipped Jim from a foot-wide ledge on the buttress above.

It was a lie, and the chain ended too soon for me, enforcing half-a-dozen steps kicked in vertical mud before I reached the comparative haven of the ledge. This was the corner buttress, poised above a tremendous view down to Fionnay and the length of the Val de Bagnes and up to all the Combins—Grand, Corbassière, and Petit. The path, still foot-wide, hairpinned round it and headed south-east at the same level along the very steep snow-streaked mountainsides under the Bec des Rosses. For two-and-a-half miles it held this course, requiring careful foot-placing all the way, and then doubled back over the saddle of a miniature col to go on just as precariously northward up the flank of a precipitous glen. The little Lac de Louvie gleamed in the corrie down on the right. At the glen-head the Col de Louvie was now in sight, a bold nick of scree and snow close under the tall crags of the Petit Mont Fort.[1]

A trickle of water down the slabs on the left where blue gentians grew on the ledges suggested lunch. When we went on an ibex watched us unconcernedly from a crag twenty feet above the path, and we saw three others as well as several marmots as we approached the col. Toilsome zigzags over stones and snow-pockets rose up the final two or three hundred feet, but there were familiar alpine flowers to soften the labour —purple mountain saxifrage, pink androsacae, gentians, and glacier crowfoot—and a chough took off from the crest as we reached it. It was 3 o'clock. A chill wind, welcome after the climb in hot sunshine, greeted us at 9,640 feet; and a splendid but somewhat daunting view. A thousand feet below, the undulant snowfield of the Grand Desert made a broad bowl tilted up to the rim of broken precipices on the south or right hand and slanting down on the north to the grey moraines at the head of the Val de Nendaz. Looking along the rank of precipices above I thought I could identify the notch of the next pass on our route, the Col de Prafleuri, to reach which we would have to cross the Grand Desert and find a way round the rock-faces. Three in the afternoon was too late to begin that venture. Since we weren't equipped for camping on snow we would have to go down to the moraines, camp there, and climb up again to the glacier next day. The prime difficulty was in getting down off the pass.

Now we beheld the result of the bad-weather spell that had just ended. Instead of the (presumably) normal declivity of rock and scree on the east side of the Col de Louvie there was an unbroken wall of snow, very steep at the top where we stood on an incipient cornice. It was a place for axes certainly,

[1] The Swiss map shows a break in the continuity of the path beyond the miniature col. It is in fact continuous.

for a rope also if you were properly cautious. We had staffs of a sort—half-rotten sticks picked up in the Verbier forests. While we peered and muttered gloomily, Alex lowered himself over the snow-edge and began to kick his way confidently down. Following gingerly, we found the snow in good condition and were soon careering down the gentler slopes on to the snow-covered glacier, which in this western half is not crevassed.

Careful reconnaissance from above here combined itself with one of my hunches and I led off downhill at a great pace, the others following willy-nilly. And in fifteen minutes from the foot of the snow-wall I halted at what, in the circumstances, could be called an ideal camp-site. This spot is just under the north flank of some humps or bluffs called on the map 'Grands Bandons', a little flat plain floored in places with springy plants that give good lying in this wilderness of rock and moraine. Five minutes away is a tarn of pure water in a hollow. The invaluable folding plastic bucket was called into service as soon as we arrived, and by 4.30 the tents were up and we were drinking the nectar known at sea-level as tea.

If this fortunate oasis had a fault, it was that the spectacular rock-faces of Petit Mont Fort soared to 10,300 feet due west of it and less than half-a-mile away, so that they had obscured the westering sun by 6.30. But the Grands Bandons sheltered it from the north wind, and hot soup proofed us against the chill of 8,500 feet. It was tomato soup with the addition of a little *rösti*, the tinned soya product obtainable throughout Switzerland, and it was followed by one slice of bread-and-butter with jam, one sweet biscuit, and one-and-a-half cups of coffee each; for a rationed meal it wasn't too bad. Jim cooked, I washed-up —an arrangement which became standard. By 8 we were in our sleeping-bags.

As I gulped the last of my antibiotics with the aid of a nubbin of chocolate I reflected that I could no longer consider myself a convalescent. After an eight-hour day of hard going and a not inconsiderable pass, carrying a heavy load, I was feeling like a million dollars. Maybe the wine-like air and the continuous sunshine had something to do with this lightning recovery. And here, perhaps, I may anticipate with the weather record of the journey. The brilliant day of the Louvie crossing was the first of nine days of sunshine, and the continuous sun of the succeeding ten days was broken only by a heavy shower near Täsch and a rainy evening at Saas Fée. Perfect weather for seventeen days of a three-week holiday is unusual in the Valais Alps and it would be rash for anyone following in our tracks to expect it. For us it soon became the expected norm; and the reader may picture the party in shirt and shorts on the rest of this journey, myself usually stripped to the waist.

It was a cold night at the Grands Bandons site, and the tents were dripping with condensation next morning. But at a quarter to seven the sun topped the eastward ridge and an hour later we were breakfasting outside in the growing warmth. Jim and I were packed and away first, pioneering a short cut to the route across the Grand Desert by striking due south up moraine and snow and slab. It was a rare delight (not without nostalgic undertones) to be kicking steps up the untrodden white crystals with the morning sun hot on one's cheek, under a sky "darkly, deeply, beautifully blue". On the broad terrace of snow and boulders above we found a huge rock with the red-and-white *Bergweg* waymark, and sat down on it to wait for the others.

The route linking the Louvie pass to the Prafleuri must be easy enough to find in ordinary summers when June and July have brought less snowfall than they did in 1974. We had to use the compass a good deal and work out the route from the features of crag and couloir, but once or twice confirmation that we were going the right way came from a glimpse of red paint at the base of a boulder which on closer examination proved to be a waymark nearly hidden under the snow. A few days after our passage, no doubt, there was a clear and continuous succession of waymarked rocks from the foot of the Louvie descent to the Prafleuri col.

At first we were following an easy line along the wide ascending shelf under the bold crags of Grande Mont Calme, walking mostly on snow. On the left was the rim of a precipice overlooking the Grands Bandons. Suddenly, however, the shelf ended and we looked steeply down into a hanging snow-cwm several hundred feet below, which offered the choice of a descent into it and out again or a nasty-looking traverse round the upper part of the steep snowslopes that dropped into it on our right. (We had seen no waymarks for some time and if there were any hereabouts they were under the snow.) The angles were such that a slip and fall from the traverse—likely enough with no axe to arrest it—could end in a further and fatal slide into the ravine at the outlet of the cwm, while a fall on the direct descent from where we stood would probably land the faller in the middle of the cwm, static and more or less alive. On the other hand, the direct descent had to begin with a clamber down some rocks projecting from the perpendicular twenty feet of snow at the top of the slope, rocks which might or might not come away at a touch.

We spent ten minutes discussing the alternatives, and then—once again—Alex showed the way. Face-inwards, using the rocks delicately and the snow more firmly, he clung down while we watched with bated breath. Everything held, and after a bout of inward-facing on the open snow-face lower down he was in the clear and kicking merrily down to the bottom. The rest of us followed and we all got down without mishap. I feel reasonably sure that in a season of less snow a waymarked route would steer the traveller less hazardously past this obstacle.

Only an easy slog up snow and splintered rock remained, and we were on the Col de Prafleuri, 9,844 feet, well before noon. It was a good moment for me. Only four miles away, on the other side of the great trough in which lay the Lac des Dix, a rank of splendid red pinnacles glowed against the blue sky— the Aiguilles Rouges d'Arolla which I had traversed in an exciting eleven-hour climb in 1951. To the right of them were Mont Collon and the Pigne d'Arolla. Such moments are as heart-warming as the reunion of old friends. Less cheering was the appearance of the descent we had now to make. Once again there was an exposed wall of snow dropping from the white cornice on the eastern rim of the Col, a quite impossible slope, and Colin and I glanced somewhat apprehensively at Alex. Would he step imperturbably over *this* edge? It was Jim, however, who found the way. A shout came from below the left-hand section of the cornice.

"The thing's easy. No problem here."

As he had discovered, the cornice abutted on a crumbling bluff—not, I am sure, the normal route of descent—and across this we tiptoed to reach a precarious scree that took us in twenty minutes to a band of level snow at the bottom. It wasn't hard, but it was a terrible come-down in another sense. For our morning of exhilarating adventure ended in an afternoon of disenchantment.

We came down into an ugly great basin of grey moraine which had been quarried for the construction of the huge dam of the Lac des Dix. Lorry-roads crossed it, ruined shacks and old iron littered it. When we had late-lunched dispiritedly beside a dirt road, our only comfort the sight of a herd of twenty bouquetin charging up and down a distant snowslope, we continued down past the old Refuge de Prafleuri and by a lesser path round a rocky bluff to a corner some hundreds of feet above the famous dam. It was impressive. A giant tanker on Wastwater would be similarly impressive. Cable-cars were hoisting tourists by the hundred from the car-park in the lower valley, sightseers strolled in crowds across the dam and prome-naded the broad track that runs along the lake's western shore, at first through a series of electrically-lit tunnels. We had seen no one at all on the passes and the sudden transition from solitude to multitude was too much for us. Striding at top speed through the throng, we outdistanced the last strolling tourist on the lakeside track and stopped only when we had gone nearly three miles along the four-mile length of the lake.

Between track and lake grassy slopes speckled with flowers hinted the possibility of a level site, and we found one below a sheltering bank beside a small stream. We pitched the tents with lightened spirits, thankful to be out of sight and sound of the tourists. . . .

How smug and silly it sounds! We ourselves were tourists, though our interest was not in hydro-electric works but in things not made with hands. Why should we grow hot and irritable at the sight and sound of men admiring the wonders created by Man? Was it, perhaps, because the arrival amongst the crowds had shattered the illusion we had created for ourselves that we were pioneering in an untravelled mountain world?

Argument and speculation (after a just-adequate supper) were interrupted by a timely discovery. The little stream a few feet from the tent doors had a loud and pleasing song when we first reached our camp-site, but now the song was so muted that we could hardly hear it. Investigation in the half-darkness

5*

revealed that the flow of water had dwindled to the merest trickle. The stream was fed from the snows of the Écoulaies glacier far overhead, and with the coming of twilight the snows had frozen. By the morning the stream-bed was as dry as a bone, but we had received the warning just in time and the plastic bucket, carefully placed below a last dribble, was half full and ready for the breakfast coffee and eggs.

It was 7.40—I was up and about to note the exact hour—when the sun lifted above the notchy Aiguilles Rouges and started dispelling the white frost from round the tents, and 8.45 when we set out in hot sunshine along the lakeside track. From the Prafleuri col we had been able to make out the position of our next pass, the Col de Riedmatten; the map, and our later observations, showed that there are alternative routes to it from the Lac des Dix. A brief topographical digression will help here.

Mont Blanc de Cheilon (12,750 feet) is the literal overseer of the long trough of the Val des Dix, and its originator too. We could see its odd pyramidal shape from the camp-site. The mountain sends its chief glacier due north down the upper part of the fifteen-mile trough between the wall of the Monts Rouges on the east and the wall of lower bluffs on the west; the lake occupies the trough's middle section and the valley north of the great dam forms the third and last part, all three parts being in a straight line south-to-north. We had entered the trough at the dam and turned south along the lake, making for the glacier. On our left, ahead, was the wall of the Monts Rouges with the Riedmatten col at its farther end, on our right was the butt-end of the lower wall of bluffs, and between them was the Glacier de Cheilon. The path to the Col de Riedmatten shown on the map keeps to the left beyond the head of the lake, as one would expect. Another path is shown going along the bluffs on the other side of the glacier and ending at the Cabane des Dix, a C.A.S. hut. The more usual way to the Riedmatten is to take this path until just short of the Cabane and then cross the glacier—almost level here and not crevassed—to the Col which is directly opposite. We were told that this route is easier than the one we used and takes less time.

Not being aware of this, we plodded along the lakeside track, rounding a sharp bend at its south-west corner. Ten minutes' walk past this corner we noted a path mounting steeply on the right; this is the path to the Cabane and probably the best way to the Col. Passing on, we came to the last abominations (or wonders) of the Val des Dix scheme. There was a suspension footbridge spanning the river that flowed into the lake from the Cheilon glacier and from it an impressive—yes, impressive—close-up view of the exit mouth of the water-tunnel. This tunnel runs beneath a dozen miles of glaciers and mountains to bring the collected water into the Lac des Dix, and it hurled it forth with a roar as if glad to be rid of it. The visual effect, however, was too reminiscent of a big laundry ejecting its detergent. Beyond the footbridge a long, steep, and glittering staircase of metal alloy climbed to a concrete box on top of a bluff. Once past this we were on a decent Alpine mountainside again—and trying to find our route.

The start of the Riedmatten path was obscure. From the south-east corner of the Lac des Dix, where we had now arrived, steeply-angled ledges separated by rock-faces rise above the true right bank of the glacier stream, and the route had to climb these somehow to get above the chaos of cliff and rock where the glacier's icefall had once been. A long zigzag left and right was indicated by the map, but the leg to the right couldn't be found. I reconnoitred an extremely narrow track that mounted grassy crags in that direction and had just decided it was a chamois track (only a chamois could have got up it) when a hail from below summoned me down again, to find that the others had discovered traces of red and white paint on a rock. Undoubtedly it was an almost obliterated *Bergweg* waymark. An unlikely-looking groove above it proved to be the path, and after this initial check the way was well marked right to the pass.

Though it was still early the sun had a noonday heat. We mounted slowly from one flowery ledge to another, noting edelweiss among many other alpine flowers, pausing frequently for "five-minuters" and taking our time; the pass was said to be an easy one and Arolla was only two hours below it. At the top of this steep section we made a longer halt for a smoke. The glacier was close ahead and well below our level, a flat pewter band in an untidy setting of jumbled grey rocks with Mont Blanc de Cheilon shining far above like a Cyclopean crystal embedded in snow. Close overhead as we sprawled among the flowers rose a buttress of bare rock, quite vertical. A chamois, skipping incautiously round a corner ledge, perceived us fifty feet below him and elected to escape by crossing the face of the buttress. He literally danced across; a miraculous sight, for though there were rugosities and convexities where one could conceive him finding foothold it was just not possible that he could keep in balance on what the old climbers used to call "an A.P. face". At any rate, his feat was an excuse for ten minutes of discussion and an extra half-pipe. But *dolce far niente* was no slogan for men who had still to cover the worst part of the Riedmatten path, which now began to traverse across the vast bank of broken rock under the wall of the Monts Rouges.

If "the sight of a horse makes the traveller lame", the sight of a nimble chamois makes the mountain backpacker stumble. We stumbled a good deal among those ankle-breaking boulders, and sweated as we stumbled. It was not a good path. Indeed, there were one or two places where it wasn't a path at all. Rock-falls from the crumbling red cliffs overhead on the left had swept it away here and there, at one point gouging across it a couloir so deep and steep that it was passable only by climbing a long way up the loose rock of one side to step perilously across and descend, equally unpleasantly, on the other. Beyond it we met a tough-looking French couple, man and woman, coming down the path with a dog. They had crossed the Riedmatten, and assured us that it was not difficult for dogs. This was comforting, as far as it went.

At 11.45 we reached the foot of the gully that leads to the Col. Less than a quarter of a mile ahead we could see the lower and steeper notch of the Pas de Chèvres, an alternative for reaching Arolla, and a party of climbers in brightly-coloured clothing descending the iron ladders which are bolted to its sheer slabs. Ladder gymnastics are not for those with heavy packs. We started up the gully, which was steep and much eroded by human passage, and reached its top at five minutes after noon.

The Col de Riedmatten, a narrow saddle in a rocky gap, had no snow on or near it though its height is 9,567 feet. We had it to ourselves except for a pair of choughs who were plainly accustomed to find their lunch in the remains of other people's.

But at the bottom of the descending zigzags on the other side there was a perspective of walkers going up and down the Arolla path in twos and threes. We scrambled down and joined the throng, to duck aside from the path for a belated lunch which lasted a great deal longer than the amount of food warranted; it was the last of the three-day ration which had kept us going for four days. It was a good place to linger, for Mont Collon was in sight above the Arolla Glacier and so were the Aiguille de la Tsa—sharpest of Aiguilles—and the Tsalion, all inviting reminiscence of a three-week guideless climbing campaign in 1951. Then our party of four had camped in a delightful spot across the river from Arolla village. There was an "official" camping-place at Arolla now, as I had discovered beforehand; but I wondered if the old site was still available.

My Log ends this day: "*Down to maintained paths, rustic bridges, and Arolla, which is much changed for the worse by droves of cars. 1951 site marked with tattered cardboard inscribed 'INTERDIT'! but we pitched there, went back to the village to shop, and celebrated three passes with a three-course dinner: ham-and-pea soup, ravioli, fruit salad. Coffee and cigar followed. 'Traviata' from the tent next door—Colin in voice tonight.*"

2. AROLLA TO GRUBEN

Arolla. Les Haudères. Col de Torrent (9,592'). Col de Sorebois (9,269'). Zinal. Pas de Forcletta (9,468'). Gruben. 4 days, 4 camps including 1 at Arolla.

I have not described our camping-place above Arolla because it appeared to be forbidden ground in 1974 and probably still is. Trespass in person may be venial but trespass by proxy is not. The permitted camping at Arolla is beside the main road ten minutes below the village, whose hotels and shops and cafés are perched on a steep hillside, and there are possible sites, also at a distance and beside a road, south of the village on the way to the Arolla Glacier. For the sybaritic or the soaked and weary there is bunkhouse-type accommodation at the pleasingly-named "Le Dortoir Sporting", which is also a restaurant and stocking-up shop.

The presence of the *INTERDIT* sign didn't disturb our sleep, but the noise of cars and vans was an annoyance in the morning. It's a long and steep hill up to Arolla and the roaring and snarling of engines is now a part of its environment. I was not surprised when Colin announced that he for one didn't want to stay another night there as we had originally thought of doing. There had been talk of spending a packless off-day walking up the track to the glacier and following it above the ice for a closer look at Mont Collon; but the track had been made into a motorable road and cars were hurtling along it in clouds of thick brown dust. Only the great mountains nudging the Italian frontier remained aloof and peaceful as of old, unchained as yet by cable-car or ski-lift, but they were not for ropeless backpackers.

So it was on again with the journey. It will have been observed that we had been able to get into the Arolla valley at its head by making our southing up the glacier in the valley west of it. It is a branch from the main Val d'Hérens, and the passes eastward into the valleys of Moiry and Zinal over the glaciers surrounding the Dent Blanche were beyond the capacity of our party. We would have to go five miles northward down the valley road before we could start climbing again to reach a practicable pass, the Col de Torrent, 9,592 feet, by which the west-east traverse could be continued into the Val de Moiry. Les Haudères at the junction with the Val d'Hérens was the launching-off place for this next pass, and the preliminary part of the ascent from Les Haudères was up another motor-road that climbed 1,500 feet to end at a place called Villa. There was no argument about how we were to do all this road-travelling. A sally into Arolla disclosed that a bus left at 11.45 for Les Haudères (there was an earlier one but we had missed it) and when it left we and our packs were on it.

Log: "*Odd how Time turns things upsy-down. 1951, Les Haudères was the crowded tourist centre and Arolla the quiet unspoilt village. 1974, positions reversed. Tourists buzz through Les H. on way to A. and the old village above the main road is what Arolla used to be like.*"

Pottering round the shops and alleys of Les Haudères in the sunshine, stocking up for the next two passes, and lunching on bread-and-cheese and peaches in a lane above the village, were all done at an off-day tempo; for there was a bus to La Sage, a mile below Villa where the path began, at 4.50 and we had an afternoon to spend. Alex spent part of it in a boot-shop. His boots had started coming apart on the Col de Prafleuri and he had crossed the Riedmatten to the rhythm of flapping soles. He bought a very good pair of Swiss boots for the equivalent of £12, but it was a mistake to change boots in mid-trip and he also paid for them in subsequent blisters.

The road to La Sage was extremely steep, the afternoon sun was extremely hot, and there was no insincerity about the usual mutual congratulations on having had the sense not to walk. The bus fare was reasonably low; but it's worth noting that Swiss buses charge as much for each pack in their luggage-trailers as they do for each passenger. Villa, like La Sage, was a modern township of neat mansions and shops with three-star views across the Val d'Hérens, a product of the boom in winter sports. Suburban paths—perhaps "superurban" would be more precise—climbed steeply away from its sophistications and after one false start we picked up a path with yellow *Wanderweg* markings and began the slog up towards the Col de Torrent. Half-past five is late in the day to set forth from a village looking for a "wild" camp-site. La Sage is at 5,500 feet and we could hardly hope to climb more than a quarter of the remaining 4,000 feet to the pass, but a camp-site we had to have. Putting on speed, we reached open mountainside sooner than expected and looked for a site. There was none. The narrow path rose gently across a very steep and stony slope with no break in it above or below. It was nearing 7 when I spotted, in a fold of mountainside ahead, a little turfy cwm with a trickle of water in it.

After six days both tent-pairs had achieved a faultless routine of tent-pitching and supper-cooking and in less than half-an-hour we were sipping chicken-and-leek soup thickened with some tinned potato-and-cheese Jim had bought in Les Haudères. Between sips we could look from the tent doorway across the dark gulf of the valley to the Arolla peaks smoking their evening pipes nine miles away. It was later and nearly dark when with a queer sense of being watched I turned to look up at the south-eastern rim of our little cwm. Jutting above the rim was a thing like the glowing red-hot tip of some

gigantic inter-stellar missile. It was the shaft of the Dent
Blanche lit by the very last of the sunset.

That camp at 6,300 feet was, I think, the coldest we had,
though we were 3,000 feet below the snowline. The north wind,
maintainer of fine weather in the Alps, made for cold nights
and there was a ground frost next morning. Still, it was the wind
that countered the blazing sun and enabled us to tramp at
speed up the zigzag path after a 9.15 start, climbing 3,000 feet
in two-and-a-half hours (good going, with the weight we had
on our backs) and arriving on the pass at 11.45. The path over
the Col de Torrent is plain and not very interesting; you could
say the same of the Col, though it does have a splendid view
towards the Weisshorn and its neighbours. Three walkers,
French, were resting on the rocky crest and we could see two
or three people coming up the track on the Moiry side, which
reminded us that the conversion of the Lac de Moiry into a
reservoir has made the Col de Torrent easily accessible as a day
excursion by car. For the motorist can reach the dam, over
7,000 feet above the sea, and cars can drive across it and along
the east shore of the lake.

"What we want to do," said Jim, "is to get off the path and
camp before we reach the lake. Then we can cross the dam
early in the morning and avoid the crowds."

(Jim detests crowds in the hills. Once when I was anathema-
tising litter he said with finality: "The worst kind of litter is
people.")

Colin, as always, was for pressing on. "Over the dam this
afternoon," he urged, "and camp well up towards the next
pass."

Alex and I sided with Jim for another reason: it was a good
drying wind for washing-day. We had been going for a week
and it was high time for a bath and change. All we needed on
a day like this was a secluded spot and a handy stream, and
we began to look for these shortly after we had halted for lunch
a thousand feet down the Moiry path.

It was a pleasant path, and not less so for the two family
parties we met coming up it through the flowery hummocks and
sunlit rocks. They stared and smiled, no doubt with good reason,
at the four men humped like Calibans who strode down the
zigzags gazing eagerly to left and to right as though looking

Camp below the Grand Desert glacier. The Col de Louvie is the nick below
the steepening of the shadowed skyline on the right

Second morning at "Camp One". Grand Combin and Petit Combin above,
Val de Bagnes below

Descent from Col de Sorebois (9,269 feet). Weisshorn, Lo Besso,
Zinal Rothhorn

Campsite on the Täschalp

Looking back at the Simeli Pass (9,916 feet) from the path to the Bistinen

On the path from the Hannig Pass to Saas Fee. Weissmies above

The Bernese Oberland seen across the Rhone Valley from the last mountain camp at 8,100 feet

for a lost sheep but in reality seeking a place to take a bath. The sea-green lake was in sight steeply below, with tomorrow's pass somewhere in the rank of high summits above its further shore, when the single-file path came down to a shelf of pasture where there were two very large barns, both deserted, beyond which it changed into a broad unmetalled track. The track curved away to the left, with about one mile of walking and five hundred feet of descent to go before reaching the dam at the north end of the lake. It was obvious that beyond this point the mountainside falling to the lake steepened considerably. If we were to camp this side the dam it would have to be here or hereabouts.

Down on the right was the stream from below the Col de Torrent, flowing through a marshy level before taking its final plunge down a ravine into the Lac de Moiry. There was no camp-ing-place by it, but it could be crossed immediately above the top of the ravine and on the other side were some craggy bluffs with what looked like a passable camp-site below them. When we got down to the place five minutes later we found that it was more than passable. A dry level sheltered from the wind was ideal for the tents, big sunwarmed boulders stood about waiting to dry the washing, and the view was a mountain-lover's dream —Pigne de la Lé, Pointe de Bricola, Grand Cornier and Dent Blanche all lifted their pale-golden snows into the blue after-noon sky. We pitched here at 3.30 and half-an-hour later were bathing and washing in the ravine. The stream came down it in a succession of leaps with small pools at the bottom of each. We took a pool each for our ablutions, presenting (to any improbable telescope on the other side of the lake) the curious spectacle of four men stripped to the buff perched one above the other at twenty-foot intervals in a vertical trough of falling water, gesticulating and reeling about; for the pool-bottoms were slippery and the water ice cold.

It was a delightful site. The "smalls" were dry and supper over when I went for an exploratory scramble to get a better viewpoint for the Dent Blanche. From a little corner buttress I saw not only the great Dent and its supporters but also—far to northward and framed in the steep walls of the Moiry valley— the Oberland peaks beyond the Rhone, Rinderhorn and Altels and Balmhorn. There, too, was the deep gap of the Gemmi Pass,

over which Colin and I had carried our packs two years ago.
But it was cold when dusk fell, for the camp was at 7,890 feet,
and there was a more comfortable pleasure to be taken over a
mug of hot bouillon in the tent, watching through the open
doorway the rose-hues fading on the high snows.

Next morning we were the only crowd on the Moiry dam
when we crossed it at 9.30. The lake is about a third as long as
the Lac des Dix but we thought the views from its curved dam
(the Dix dam is straight) were more impressive, the distant
Oberland in the north and the beautiful Moiry glacier to
southward. At the eastern end of the dam a neat hut for the
sale of picture postcards and sweets was not yet open. Directly
above it a path, or earthy staircase, mounted to open hillsides
beyond, where we threaded a way through a large herd of cows
and calves, every one of them wearing a bell and apparently
rooted to the ground. One or two of the calves decided we were
"finger-lickin' good". This route turned out to be a short-cut
to the upper zigzags of an old bridle-track that began a little
farther on along the dam road and ended a few zigzags after
we joined it. There was no indication that this was the right
way to the Col de Sorebois, the 9,269-foot pass by which we
intended to get into the Val de Zinal, and the steep and narrow
path that climbed on northward, instead of eastward towards
the crest on our right, kept us in doubt until it reached the
saddle above a buttress overlooking the Val de Moiry, a
magnificent viewpoint. Here it swung sharply to the east and
climbed the last thousand feet by zigzags and a final scree-slope
to the pass.

There is one of Colin's photographs to show the view that
confronted us. If it wasn't for this splendid prospect the Col de
Sorebois could be called a disappointing pass, even an ugly
one. It is said that Tennyson, on being shown the Grindelwald
glacier, remarked: "That is a filthy thing. It looks as though a
thousand London seasons had passed over it." He might have
said the same about the upper slope of the Sorebois on the
Zinal side. The surface of the slope had the chewed-up
appearance of a football field on the outskirts of a colliery
town. Across it marched the pylons of ski-lifts. Under them
were aimless rutted tracks which the short grass was struggling
to cover, suggestive of a building estate planned but never

started. A less obscure track with one or two people walking up it ran below the pass to mount to the rounded ridge above it leading to the Corne de Sorebois (9,590 feet) where we descried a large shack which could have been a restaurant or the top station of a cable-car line.

Mentally donning blinkers, we looked only at the splendours of the Besso and the Zinal Rothorn as we hurried down easy slopes—once of turf but now miserably shaven by the spring skiers—to the broad track. Colin's heart had been greatly uplifted by the fact that we were over this pass before noon, but we applied the brake to his onward rush towards Zinal and halted to lunch by a stream as soon as the horrible slope was above us. When we started down again it was by so beautiful a path that the higher abominations were soon forgotten.

One of the things—perhaps the chief thing—that makes backpacking over high passes so satisfying is the swift contrast experienced. Variety is certainly the spice of life but the exciting taste is lost unless the changes occur at short intervals, and mountain backpacking arranges this for you in several ways. There is your night's lodging, for instance. Towards late afternoon you are usually aloft on the shelterless barrens; half-an-hour later you are at home in a snug tent with tea on the brew. With the scenery it's the same. The transition from the bare bones of the ridges to the softer splendours of the lower lands comes so rapidly that appreciation is whetted and the full flavour of Earth's varied delights makes a memorable impression. From the foot of the desolate upper slopes of the Sorebois down to Zinal the path descends 3,000 feet in an endless series of zigzags, and at every turn you come upon a new and lovelier vista—banks of brilliant flowers under steeps of greenery with horns of grey crag jutting from them, the background at one corner the blues and greens of the valley floor and at the next the far glitter of snow-peak and glacier. Only the descent to St Niklaus from the Augstbord Pass, as I remember it, can compete with this path for sheer beauty. But Zinal—my Log has a word for it: *"A final ½-mile of busy motor road to the sprawling Saturday-spree township of Zinal, all cars and people and souvenir shops."*

We spent an hour in Zinal because Jim had to make a phone call to North Wales on urgent business. While he was at it we replenished our stores for the next pass, the Pas de Forcletta over to Gruben in the Turtmanntal. On the map Gruben looked a very small place indeed, so we were careful to lay in sufficient food and Camping Gaz to see us over the succeeding pass beyond which were the ample supplies of the Zermatt valley. Besides some flowery hotel gardens, I remember one pleasanter sight in Zinal: a file of a dozen or more tiny children in charge of two adults, steering through the busy street aided by a thirty-foot rope with one of the adults at each end and the children holding on to it between them.

Precipitous forests rise straight above Zinal on the west, and a path, its start in the town not easy to find, mounts steeply up them. A *Bergweg* waymark on a wall near the church is the clue. It is not a path devoted solely to the Forcletta pass but a link with the long network of high-level paths that reaches right along the flank of the south-to-north ridge on the west side of the Val d'Anniviers. Ayer, in the valley three miles north of Zinal, is the proper base for a direct crossing of the Forcletta, and Gruben in the Turtmanntal is two miles north of the Forcletta. Our course was therefore to be a dog-leg one: a long traverse north on the Anniviers flank, a crossing of the pass due west, and another northerly traverse to come down to Gruben. Once again we felt the disadvantages of a late-afternoon start uphill for a camp-site. To begin another climb at 4.30 p.m. after the crossing of a high pass puts an added burden on one's bulging pack, and the charms of the path—in its higher reaches a scenic one—could only be appreciated at occasional halts to rest. One or two descending walkers were encountered in the forest but well before the path's emergence on open mountainside at 7,000 feet it was deserted. As on the flank below the Col de Torrent two days earlier, no possible camp-site presented itself for some time; and it was after 7 when the path, a broad and plain one, ended a long horizontal traverse by curling into and out of the deep ravine of a torrent. Above the ravine and well back from the path we found a perch for the tents where some massive rocks stood on a shelf thigh-deep in grass and flowers. It was not a comfortable site. Anything dropped in the jungle of grass was lost irretrievably and it was a long and precarious way down to the ravine to fetch water. But we spent a warm night there and woke to early sunshine. The long grass was soaking wet and Jim and I breakfasted squatting like Copenhagen mermaids on the slanting top of a rock above the green sea.

The traversing path that had seemed dull and featureless the previous evening was beautiful in the clear morning after a night's rest. Orchis and other flowers bordered it, and looking back from a corner we had a first glimpse of the distant Matterhorn stabbing into the blue sky behind the forked Besso and the Gabelhorn ridges. This path was oddly frequented. We met first one and then another man *running* along it, attired in a mixture of mountain gear and gent's athletic wear, and when we left the path to strike easterly up the slope we could see other runners on it below. We learned later that they were taking part in a sort of annual marathon from St Luc to Zinal.

Muirhead's *Blue Guide* had called the Pas de Forcletta "interesting" and added "guide 25 fr.", so we expected something better than the Sorebois. We were not disappointed. The westerly branch track, small but fairly well waymarked, climbed to an upper cwm where there was a herd of Simmental cows and then up the wall of the cwm to steep scree and the pass, which was reached at noon precisely. The narrow rock crest between horns of rock, 9,468 feet up, was a great deal more like an Alpine pass than the Sorebois, and a place to linger in for its views of peaks and valley in spite of a penetrating north wind. Two small parties of climbers were up there, and when after a 45-minute halt we began the descent we met half-a-dozen others, including a middle-aged Englishman with an ice-axe—the first of our fellow-countrymen to be encountered in nine days of travel. His axe wasn't unnecessary, for we had come down two steep slopes of snow in poor condition just below the crest. Lunch on a carpet of blue gentians beside a stream supplemented the snack eaten among the sheltering crags of the pass. And it wasn't more than an hour later when we came down a steep of zigzags to a broad and beautiful shelf of the mountainside where a stream meandered lazily across levels of grass and flowers between old moraine mounds clothed with verdure. Beyond the edge of the shelf rose a shining rank of peaks, and the Weisshorn, loveliest of mountains, brandished a white blade of summit aloft in the south. It was 2.45 p.m. and a debate ensued.

"Much too early to camp, man! Why, we could get past Gruben and halfway to the next pass."

"Fagged out, same as yesterday? No—and I want to shave before we meet the Grubenites."

"It'll put us a day behind."

"Who cares? This is an ideal site, the view's a world-beater, and—well, camping in places like this is what backpacking's about."

The early-stoppers carried the day and we pitched the tents in that delightful place. This, to my mind, *is* what backpacking is about. It's a way of travel with many advantages, including the unique one of being able to halt, dine, and sleep where the splendours of our world are most marvellously displayed. We cooked and shaved, scribbled in diaries and patched blisters; and when we lifted our eyes from these mundane tasks there was always the vision of mountain beauty gleaming like the pillars of heaven beyond the more earthly pastures in front of the tents. I doubt whether there is a more spiky panorama to be seen in the Alps than this view across the Turtmanntal from the Forcletta descent. Every peak is a Horn—Stellihorn, Barrhorn, Brunegghorn, Bishorn, Weisshorn.

It was the Weisshorn that won the beauty-contest, as might be expected. Supper was over and we were out for a last stroll in the dusk before turning in. All the other peaks looked grey and old, but the Weisshorn was glowing with an incredibly brilliant ruby light. We watched it for a while, but the evening wind of the heights was penetratingly cold. I had picked up some pieces of dry wood as we walked, so we lit a fire and warmed our rumps before a blaze brighter than the fading glow on the Weisshorn.

The start next morning was early enough to satisfy Colin that the party wasn't entirely dedicated to the conservation of energy. The sun, again in a cloudless sky, struck the tents at 5.30 a.m., and two hours later we were on our way down to Gruben. The paths remembered as delightful on this journey were always the downhill ones; probably there is a reason for this. The descent to Gruben was another of them, partly because the Turtmanntal, as its quiet beauty was unfolded below us, looked unspoiled and uncommercialised. Log: "*I think the Turtmanntal the most charming valley we've yet seen. The*

Weisshorn at the head of it looks stupendous, and the Turtmann Glacier is a marvel, all icefalls." There is a motorable lane up this valley but it is much less busy than the Val d'Hérens roads, and the village of Gruben (or Meiden—the two hamlets merge into one another) is more like a Swiss village of the Golden Age of mountaineering than any other we passed through.

We were in Gruben at 9 o'clock and the first customers in its very small but well-stocked store. They had no Camping Gaz cartridges here, but we had enough to last us to the Zermatt valley. A pint of milk per man—as always when it was available—a leisurely pipe, and away at 10.

This day, July 29th, we were halfway on the twenty-day journey, with eleven days in hand.

3. GRUBEN TO ZERMATT

Gruben. Augstbord Pass (9,492'). St Niklaus. Täschalp. Zermatt. 4 days, 4 camps, including 1 extra day and camp at the site above Zermatt.

The man who has no music in his soul is at a disadvantage for uphill backpacking. Nothing (for me, at least) is such a help when humping a load up a very steep slog as the iteration of a good rhythmic tune. Bach has lots of them, and a two-part fugue can be managed if you hum the tune mentally instead of aloud. I was passing through a Mozart phase in 1974 and whistled the third movements of piano concertos on the climb out of Gruben; breathing at the same time as whistling is no problem if you whistle on the intake as well as on the blowout.

There is no nonsense about the path from Gruben to the Augstbord Pass. It starts from the middle of the Gruben/Meiden chalets and swarms straight up forested crags by innumerable zigzags to the open mountainside where the angle eases somewhat. Still making direct for the pass, due east, it follows a little tumbling stream until this vanishes under the final abrupt steepening into a glacis of rock and scree which at the time of our passage had still some patches of snow on it. The others were well ahead of me when I reached the foot of the glacis. It was half-past twelve and nearly six hours since I'd eaten any solid food. In my experience, hill-walkers and backpackers vary a great deal as to the length of time they can go without refuelling the body, and in my own case fatigue and a certain moroseness are invariable indications that the last meal was five hours ago and more food is needed. Leaving the other three to achieve 3,500 feet in two-and-a-quarter hours and lunch on the pass, I sat down on a warm rock and lunched beside the flower-bright springs of the stream.

I spent an hour basking and eating by the stream, and the pause for food suggests a pause here to explain for the possible benefit of other backpackers what our often-mentioned "stocking up" entailed.

Each tent foraged separately. By now it had been discovered that individual tastes fitted handily into the present arrangement and no one wanted to swap partners. Colin and Alex had similar tastes in basic food, Jim and I preferred coffee to the tea or Oxo favoured by the other two. Apart from the bread and eggs common to both tents, we shopped in couples and picked what we wanted. Breakfast was standard—boiled egg, bread-and-butter, jam, and a hot drink. Lunch was basically bread and cheese and a tomato; the only safe place for carrying a tomato, incidentally, is in one's drinking-mug. Supper was a good big boiling of packet soup, Knorr-Swiss or Maggi, bread, biscuits and jam, and tea or coffee, the soup being supplemented on the first night out from a stock-up by a tin of ravioli or something similar. All these things could be obtained at any Swiss township that boasted a store. Towards the end of the trip we were getting very choosy about the soups and biscuits, and carrying more of the sweets and chocolate (the cheap slabs of cooking-chocolate much preferred) for nibbling at intervals. On paper the calorie-content of this diet looks shockingly inadequate, and I dare say six weeks on it would have proved it so. But we did twenty days of hard work on it and finished fitter than fighting-cocks. Lots of liquid, plenty of sugar, and a sufficiency of salt were the essentials for the sort of life we were leading.

The *Blue Guide* (1953) gives the guide's fee for the Augstbord Pass as 40 francs—easy money, I opined at first. The pleasantly narrow crest between Schwarzhorn and Rothorn is easy and straightforward to gain from the west, and though the descent on the east is quite steep there is no difficulty. I don't think anyone could miss the way even in thick weather if he had a map. After my halt for replenishment I climbed the last 500 feet without stopping and joined the others in their chilly nook on the col. As usual, the views were magnificent, but we were getting rather *blasé* about magnificent views and began the descent five minutes after my arrival, by noisy zigzags down loose rock and scree varied by the crossing of a snow-runnel or two. In a snow-filled hollow at the bottom of this section half-a-dozen sheep were reclining contentedly in the snow, possibly anticipating their end as frozen mutton.

Though you climb only 3,500 feet from Gruben to the Augstbord, it's more than 5,000 feet down to St Niklaus on the other side. Even our thrusters agreed that there was no point in travelling on after 4, and as soon as we were well down among the grassy hummocks we began looking for a level site with a convenient stream. Mountains always, but valleys rarely, provide a good site when you want one. We pitched at 3.30 in a picturesque nook below a precipice of black rock down which a wisp of waterfall splashed, a place whose advantage of openness to the east—so that it would get the early-morning sun—was balanced by equal openness to the north and the cold and searching wind. Below it, in the direction of tomorrow's journey, the ground fell away in forbidding steeps and we didn't at once perceive how we were to get down. However, a scramble across to the waterfall to fill the plastic bucket revealed *Bergweg* waymarks traversing southward round a precipitous corner. It looked an interesting route.

There was a slight *contretemps* here, more amusing to the Itisa than to the Good Companions. The latter tent was out of sight of its neighbour behind a big rock. Colin and Alex dashed off to take photographs of the distant Mischabel peaks while Jim and I brewed coffee under the close inspection of three belled sheep, which I finally drove away with execrations and stones. When the photographers returned it was to find that the sheep had entered their tent and eaten a concoction of soup-powder and ravioli left ready for cooking in a saucepan.

Unexpectedly, this camp at 8,200 feet was the warmest and most comfortable night yet. Expectedly, the sun was on the tents by 6. Exhorted by Colin, the party was under way at 8 sharp, crossing the foot of the waterfall stream to thread a waymarked way through a maze of fallen boulders. It was a gloriously clear morning.

The upper part of the descent path from this point made me think more tolerantly of the guide's 40-franc fee. It was spectacular—extremely so—and not without route-finding problems; more a rock traverse than a path, winding across the faces of broken crags and along snow-covered shelves to round an abrupt corner of precipice. It had been newly waymarked with dabs of red paint, but in one place at least a recent rockfall had swept across the marked route and left a steep and crumbling ravine which had to be crossed by a rickety traverse higher up. The corner provided a sudden and breathtaking view into the Zermatt valley 3,000 feet below, and of the peaks —Nadelhorn, Dom, Monte Rosa, Castor, Pollux, Breithorn, Klein Matterhorn—ranged above the narrow green valley flanked with grey crags and hanging forests. An hour below this viewpoint we came to a good but steep mule-track dropping in zigzags down the precipitous scarps above St Niklaus. Exhilarated no doubt by the bit of near-mountaineering we'd just done, my companions sped down the mule-track like rolling stones, while I—a confirmed moss-gatherer—fell behind in the course of admiring the "quaint enamell'd eyes" of wayside flowers. Thinking I'd better catch up with the others before they entered St Niklaus, I put on speed, rashly continuing to accelerate at a place where the unfenced track slanted down at a very high angle across a rock-face, its surface the bare bedrock from which it had been carved. The rounded pebble I failed to notice acted like a roller-skate. There was an instant of much increased acceleration and I finished a dozen feet lower down the path, flat on my back with my legs sticking out over the verge of the very considerable drop below. I mention this incident to point the fact that it isn't only on the tricky traverse high up that the laden backpacker needs to watch his step.

We got down to St Niklaus at noon. Four hours of fast going down rocky paths had done Alex's new-boot blisters no good and we were all tired and footsore; slogging uphill with a heavy pack is trying to the wind, but pounding downhill is far more trying to the muscles. Of St Niklaus we saw little except the railway station. The path from the Augstbord Pass comes down to the station of the Visp-Zermatt narrow-gauge railway, which is a little above the town and the car-infested main road, and since the canopies of the station platform offered shade from the intensely hot sunshine we lunched there, washing down the last of our rations with water from the station tap. Though a token discussion took place it was really a foregone conclusion that we would take the train to Täsch.

To visit Zermatt at the head of the Mattertal required the longest up-valley divergence of our journey. The route west-to-east by the walking passes continues from St Niklaus by crossing the easy Hannig Pass into the Saastal, which meant that we had to go north twelve miles up the valley to Zermatt and then back again to St Niklaus. A high-level approach to Zermatt was on our programme: from the village of Täsch up to the Täschalp at about 7,500 feet and thence by a mountainside path to the heights east of Zermatt. For this we had first to reach Täsch, a seven-mile walk up a main road with no alternative for the pedestrian—a prospect rendered even more discouraging by the ceaseless roar of cars passing through St Niklaus on their way to Täsch. So we got on the little train (there is one about every one-and-a-half hours) and got out of it twenty minutes later at Täsch.

Täsch was a car-park, probably the biggest in Switzerland. Zermatt's excellent plan of keeping its narrow streets free from cars means that all motorists have to park at Täsch and go on by the railway, and the result in 1974 was a vast mass of ranked cars extending right across the valley, very nearly from one side to the other, an eyesore to anyone but a director of General Motors or a car-park attendant. I was told later that the Zermatt authorities are to solve the problem by blasting a Cyclopean cavern into the mountainside nearer their village; it will be a pretty sight to see the motorists vanishing into this like the rats in the Pied Piper story. There is a village, neither very attractive nor very Swiss, on the edge of the Täsch car-park, and here we stocked up for two camps, anticipating that we might be late arriving at the "official" Zermatt camp-site where we intended to stay in two days' time. The store had been an *épicerie* at Arolla. Here it was a *Konsumverein*, for we had crossed into a German-speaking part of the Valais, but the serve-yourself system is usual in most Swiss shops dealing with tourists and there's no language difficulty when you simply collect what you want and dump it in front of the cashier. When we started for the Täschalp at 3 a thundery haze had spread over the sky and it was hotter than ever.

Our map (the current *Landeskarte*, Sheet 284) didn't mark the new motorable road that runs from Täsch to its autonomous Alp and this helped to make the next three hours less than enjoyable. The old path can still be used to short-cut the lacets of the mounting road, but after the walk of the morning this was like cooking-sherry after Tio Pepe. The one alleviation was a backward view of the Matterhorn, looking extra huge in the thickening haze and with woolly clouds hanging round its base. The last uphill mile of road had taken over the path, and the 'ammer, 'ammer, 'ammer on the 'ard 'ighway had become almost too much for us when it was relieved by the end of the road at a few chalets and a chapel and we could tread a turfy track that went on up the somewhat bare and featureless glen. Alex and Colin were far ahead, no doubt in search of a camping-place out of sight of the road half-a-mile below. I was past caring for such niceties. There was flat grass and a trickle of water close at hand, and we pitched the Itisa then and there and lit the stove for a brew of tea that was sorely needed.

Across the lower valley the Weisshorn loomed through the haze, a pallid ghost above pallid glaciers. Perhaps it was the gloom and the heavy atmosphere that makes this Täschalp site, in memory, the least attractive of our Valais camp-sites. It was, however, the warmest. And the morning was very warm, with intermittent sun breaking through clouds. Having made contact with the other two a quarter of a mile up the glen, Jim and I were away at 9.30 without waiting for them.

The traversing path we followed towards Zermatt is magnificent but not mountaineering. It leads off round the corner south-west from the upper Täschalp chalets at 7,200 feet and keeps at this height for seven miles, with the Zermatt valley below on the right and an array of fine peaks across the 3,000-foot gulf. On this warm thundery morning the Matterhorn was swathed in cotton-wool cloud, but the Weisshorn was clear and had an impressive plume blowing off its curving east ridge. The path itself had been made safe for democracy by what appeared to be a recent carving-out with a miniature bulldozer, and on any place where Grandma or little Willy might conceivably trip and fall over the edge elaborate new railings of glittering alloy had been erected. Plainly we were within the bounds of *Grande Tourisme*.

The threatened thunderstorm broke at last when we reached a craggy corner overlooking the massed hotels of Zermatt. The thunder was distant but the rain at close quarters and heavy. Dodging across the front of the crag, I found a narrow cleft where a flake had split away from the main mass and we crammed uncomfortably into it to while away the storm with lunch. Alex and Colin appeared on the path below just as the rain stopped; they had crossed the shoulder of the Sattelspitz to the traversing path, a more mountainy route than ours. The reunited party moved on in brightening weather, which did not (if my Log is to be trusted) do much to brighten our view of the Zermatt scene: *"Path wide and much-trodden. Exchanged greetings with several family parties in gay attire. The mountain ridges on the left and in front were dreary with wires and gantries, with cable-cars and newly-made jeep roads. A helicopter kept grinding up and down the valley and there was litter along the path. Only the cloud-hooded Matterhorn preserved the legendary splendour of Zermatt—and not far to the left of the Matterhorn a line of pylons and wires made a black streak on the snows of the Théodule."*

The high-level path above the east side of the upper Mattertal ends on the sharp corner of mountainside formed by the deep Findeln glen, which cuts eastward as it rises to the Findeln glacier. On the corner, called Sunegga, is a restaurant and a bathing-pool, with a cable-car station above. A favourite ploy with the more energetic Zermatt visitors is to ascend to Sunegga by cable-car and walk down, and a good path descends straight to Zermatt 2,300 feet below by which we could have reached the metropolis of the Mattertal by 4 o'clock. By common consent we turned away from the downward path. It was only too plain that if this part of the Valais was to keep us in the state to which we were accustomed we would have to get farther away from Zermatt. A much smaller path mounted due east from near the bathing-pool and by this we began to climb into the higher part of the Findeln alp.

Sydney Smith once described Switzerland as "an inferior sort of Scotland", and certainly the Swiss appear to have the same highly-developed sense of propriety as the Scots. The bathing-pool (in reality it is a small natural lake called the Leissee) was completely deserted when we passed it, and its use by bathers was revealed only by two neat dressing-rooms constructed of green canvas and labelled respectively FRAUEN and HERREN; they were situated on opposite sides of the lake.

With our backs to Zermatt we toiled up that very steep path and were delighted to be making for the heights again. It does seem that 8,000 feet above the sea is the place to seek the ideal camp-site in the Pennine Alps; and at a little above this height we found one. The path, which is the route to the Fluhalp Hut from which the Rimpfischhorn and the peaks of the Weissgrat are climbed, contoured the steep flank below the Unterrothorn and in half-an-hour from the Leissee was traversing above another small lake. Cutting downhill and along the rocky lake shore, we ascended a hundred feet or so and found ourselves in a charming spot that had everything we could have hoped for. It was a narrow glen of level turf, a Pyrenean *jasse* in miniature. On one side it was flanked by the mountainside, on the other by a bank of boulders and thickets topped by scattered pines. A waterfall tumbled down a rock step at its head and its open western end commanded a picture-postcard view of the little tree-fringed lake—the Grindjisee—whose still waters reflected the Matterhorn in its most impressive aspect. The waterfall stream curled through the grass and flowers near the boulder-bank and we pitched the tents there at 4. No sooner were Squatters' Rights ratified by the inevitable cuppa than a roll of thunder heralded the start of light but steady rain that continued for the rest of the evening.

We didn't in fact see the Matterhorn from the Grindjisee site until next morning, for it was wrapped in dense cloud when we arrived there. Nothing, of course, can alter the singularity of the Matterhorn. But the endless repetition of its shape in photographs, postcards, posters and advertisements has made it almost tiresomely familiar, so that after the first impact I felt that I was looking at an example of mass-production. The great pinnacle was indeed superb on that clear blue morning, glistening with new snow and (one might fancy) gazing admiringly down at its perfect reflection in the Grindjisee, like

Narcissus. Yet I didn't regret the occasion when I had wanted to traverse the Matterhorn and the rest of the party had opted for the Dent Blanche instead. And I wondered, as I looked at its graceless angularity, whether Edward Whymper ever returned to the opinion he recorded in his journal when he saw the Matterhorn for the first time: "What precious stuff Ruskin has written about this, as well as about many other things! The Matterhorn may be compared to a sugar-loaf set up on a table. The sugar-loaf should have its head knocked on one side."

While we were breakfasting outside in the sun on a bank of turf and juniper, a family of marmots played merrily outside their burrow on the opposite hillside, aware of our near presence but obviously careless of it. The murmur of the water-fall at the valley-head came and went on a gentle breeze that set the flowers dancing beside the little Findel Bach a few yards from the tents. Even with Colin singing *Your tiny hand is frozen* this wilderness were Paradise enow—or would have been if we'd had the loaf of bread and the jug of wine. Two soup-packets and a few biscuits were all the food that remained after breakfast, and if we camped another night here as we had unanimously decided to do supplies would have to be brought up from Zermatt. I volunteered to do this on condition that I came up with my packages on the Sunegga cable-car, the cost of the ride being shared equally by all. I was further commis-sioned to locate and report on an official camp-site in Zermatt; we could manage one more day here and from a valley camp we might get in a walk to the Schönbühl Hut or even up to the Hörnli.

A broad and scenic path goes down from the Leissee past the Findeln chalets to Zermatt. The descent with an empty sack took me one-and-a-quarter hours going at a cracking pace, and I met a great many people (over 100, for at that number I stopped counting) coming up the lower zigzags, which were inches deep in dust. And so, by an illegal short cut across the Gornergrat Railway, into Zermatt, the Mecca of the moun-taineer. The place is tersely described in my Log: "*Zermatt now too large to be romantic. Streets hot and crowded—tourists dressed as for beach or cocktail-bar. Everything v. expensive. Beer 30p. per small bottle.*"

For lunch I ate bread-and-cheese and two small cakes in a hayfield half-an-hour's walk above the town.

4. ZERMATT TO SAAS FÉE

Zermatt. St Niklaus–Grächen. Hannig Pass (7,064'). Saas Fée. 3 days, 3 camps, including 2 camps at one site.

William Tell never was. So say modern historians, who main-tain that the legendary crossbowman's apple-splitting feat was lifted bodily out of a Scandinavian saga. So it's no longer Tell's Day on August 1st but Swiss National Day.

It was Thursday August 1st when I entered Zermatt as representative of the Pennine Alps Backpacking Expedition, and the banks and the post office were consequently closed; though everything else was open and busy, including a large multiple store called *VÉGÉ* where I did the necessary stocking up. The well-weighted pack made the cable-car lift very welcome and the subsequent foot-slog up to the Grindjisee tiring, but it was pure delight after the crowds and heat of the valley to return to the idyllic site above the lake.

It will have been noted that our Grindjisee camp-site, though high and secluded, was not really remote from the sophisticated area round Zermatt. There was a small notice-board near the farther end of the lake requesting people not to pick flowers. It was the only sign of conservation, but it is just possible that camping hereabouts is frowned upon by the local authority. We never bothered to find out.

While I had been pottering among the fleshpots Colin and Alex had been bathing, shaving, photographing and strolling. Jim, more energetic, had found his way across the moraines to the path climbing to the Gornergrat, achieving a height of 10,289 feet and gaining—with a rail-borne multitude—the most famous viewpoint in the Alps. When we had feasted royally on peaches and onion soup, fruit salad and coffee and cigar, it was felt that something should be done to celebrate National Day. We could have done with Brad Herzog's zeal for log-carrying, displayed in the Pyrenees the previous year; but Alex and Colin between them collected enough wood for a tolerable bonfire and at 8 p.m. a fine blaze in our Findeln glen answered the red fire-specks that glowed on the Hörnli ridge.

I had inspected and reported on the two camp-sites in Zermatt. The "official" one was near the station, noisy and crowded. The other, at Blatten, was half-an-hour uphill from the centre of Zermatt, and though pleasantly enough situated was nearly full of close-sited tents on ground beaten hard and denuded of grass by successions of campers. When we got down to it at 10 next morning Colin took an instant dislike to it; and indeed it was a slum after our Dorchester above the Grindjisee. There was a debate. Chance our luck higher up on the path to the Schwarzsee, or get down to St Niklaus and continue the journey? St Niklaus won the day and we plodded down into the thronging streets of Zermatt to change travellers' cheques and lunch on beer and pastries. At 12.23 the little train rattled away from Zermatt station with four impatient backpackers on board. Crowds, wheels, and rails couldn't be left behind too soon for us, and we were determined to camp that night on or near our next eastward pass.

The Hannig Pass isn't really a pass at all. The long crest of peaks stretching north from the Dom, highest summit in Switzerland, ends in a sharp promontory above Stalden, where Mattertal and Saastal meet to continue down to the Rhone Valley as the Visptal. Until it reaches this promontory under the 8,000-foot Wannenhorn the crest presents no pass that can be crossed without genuine mountaineering, and the first opportunity for the walker of getting into the Saastal is a path that mounts from the village of Grächen above St Niklaus to curl round under the northern steeps of the Wannenhorn on to the flank of the next valley. At 7,064 feet this would be by far the lowest of our passes—below the treeline, in fact—and the map marked a cable-car line running up to it. However, we would doubtless find a place to camp in the forest, on the pass or just beyond it.

In St Niklaus the heat was tropical. We had no qualms of conscience about getting on the bus that was about to leave the station for Grächen, 2,000 feet up the lacets of a busy car road. On the map Grächen looked the sort of village where stocking-up facilities would be available. When we reached it Grächen

6

was a large modern township geared to all the needs of summer residents and winter-sporters, and it was in a big supermarket that we did our stocking up before filing grimly past the hotels and chairlifts and new chalets to the start of the Hannig path. Beginning as a steep road, the path climbed through woods as a broad lane down which many holiday-makers were romping gaily; but the throng thinned out and the way steepened higher up, finally becoming a shale slope a hundred yards wide where it had been converted into a *piste* for the winter skiers. Above this we arrived dispiritedly, at 4.15, on a large grass terrace occupied by buildings, a cable-car station and a restaurant among them. It was the top of the "pass". We sat down on a bank below the restaurant to nibble chocolate and discuss the situation. Precipitous forest rose at the back of the terrace—no water there and probably no level place to camp. There were flat places between the buildings and no doubt the restaurant would give us some water, but the idea of pitching the tents here was repellent. The decision to go on along the path and camp by the first water set us on our way more hopefully, past a signpost that said "SAAS FEE 5 STD". There were three hours of daylight left and obviously it was impossible to cover the five-hour distance to Saas, but we were confident that a site with water would present itself within an hour at most. The Hampstead Heath neighbourhood of the pass was hardly out of sight behind us when the path, suddenly narrowing, swerved sharply to the right on a brow of steep forest and *presto!* everything was changed.

It was a surprising transformation. Instead of multitude there was solitude; instead of sunshine there was deep shadow; and instead of marching two-and-two on a broad track we were sidling in single file along a ledge overhanging a precipice. Nearly 4,000 feet below us—very steeply below—was the river at the bottom of the narrow Saastal, a pale thread in the dark-blue depths. Every peak on the ridge south of the Wannenhorn sends down a face of unbroken steepness into the Saas valley, and we were now committed to a long high-level traverse across all those faces. In Saas later on we learned that this route is known as the *Hohenweg* and that its accomplishment is considered a meritorious feat for walkers.

The path, a foot wide and no more, climbed steep corners

with verticality below and above, clung in and out of gullies like lift-shafts, crept precariously under overhangs where the scrape of your pack on the rock overhead threatened to tip you over the edge and on down. Balance was often a tricky business with a bulky pack, so steep was the rock-wall on the right and so exiguous the footing for edging past it. It was really superb going, with the snows of Fletschhorn and Lagginhorn and Weissmies golden in mid-air on the left, high above the darkening trench of the valley; but camp-site there was none, nor water either. Log: "*It went on and on, just the same. Nowhere where you could sit down to rest, let alone camp—and not one trickle of water down the immense clefts and rock-walls.*" Half-past five, and no sign of anything but precipice. On we clambered, glad of the fixed iron rail at two hair-raising places. Six o'clock. A very high blade of cliff, perpendicular, seemed to forbid all further progress until we came closer and found that the path passed through it by way of a tunnel eight feet long.

"It's getting late. What about a bivvy in the tunnel?"

"There's no water. Let's give it another chance—round the next corner."

But round the next corner was a grim couloir coming down the face of the Seetalhorn, whose walls we tiptoed round like beetles in a lavatory-pan. On the nose beyond it there were some rock-ledges big enough for one man to lie on. Dusk was already falling, for the sky had clouded over and a light drizzle was cooling our faces; the suggestion that we should occupy a ledge each for the night was seriously discussed. But I had one of my hunches.

"One more corner. By the pricking of my thumbs, there's a good site just round it."

The site wasn't just round the corner. But easier ground was—a rock slope instead of sheer cliffs—and for the first time in two hours the path made a descent lasting more than two minutes. It was descending across the wide mouth of a couloir, and overhead, above a rock step in the narrows of the cleft, we could see the grey-green icefall of the Ferich Glacier. The bottom of the couloir flattened out below us before the glacier stream took its final plunge into the Saastal, and a few hundred feet down the torrent there was what looked like a possible site. However unsuitable it might be it would have to do, for it was beginning to get dark. We clattered at speed down the rocks of the path and turned off it to reach the lower couloir.

In five minutes it was made clear that the hunch had been a good one. Though the glacier torrent was milky and unfit for drinking there was a brook of pure water a few yards from it. The brook had its source in a pine-clad boulder slope where there was unlimited wood for a fire if we needed one. The possible site turned out to be two excellent tent emplacements on level patches of turf sheltered by boulders as big as cottages, handy to the torrent for washing up and looking eastward (for early-morning sun) to a superb view of the glacier-hung Böshorn and Fletschhorn. The tents were pitched in a twinkling and by 8 we were dining in comfort, with candle-light to add the touch of luxury and the glacier stream providing music.

I doubt whether life offers anything more satisfying than moments like these; when, after effort and uncertainty and a chance taken, you find a snug corner in the wilds and make your home there.

It was a marvellous place to be, as we saw in the clear sunshine of next morning. Except where the tents were established the surrounding landscape was all rugged verticalities. Crags with pine trees clinging to them framed the snow-peaks across the valley to eastward, walls of shattered rock soared on either hand, jagged pinnacles at the upper end of the couloir supported a just-seen glacier and a scallop of snow-ridge far above. Jim thought it more Pyrenean than Alpine, and indeed it was reminiscent of one of the higher *jasses* under the Franco-Spanish frontier. The proposition that this was the place to spend our spare day, the day we hadn't spent at Zermatt, was carried without opposition: chiefly, I think, because the grandeur of the place had taken hold on us and it seemed a sin to hurry away from it.

For Jim and me that off-day was a memorable one, though neither of us went far from the tents. My memories of it are nearly all sensory ones. The feel of hot sun and cool breeze, the gasping chill of the torrent pool where I bathed, the warm roughness of the huge boulder that gave a twenty-foot climb; the rumble of the stream close at hand among its rocks and the faint, far music of its fall below the glacier; the shape and colour of shattered buttresses soaring above the pinewoods, and the green ice jewel-bright against the blue sky overhead. But I also washed shirt and socks and clambered in the steep forest among great bushes of alpenrose in full bloom. Meanwhile Alex and Colin had gone off with our ten-metre perlon line to attempt an ascent of the glacier to the ridge above it. They got up the glacier—Colin putting a leg into a crevasse on the way— but had to retreat from a very loose wall of rock below the ridge. A fire of pine and juniper kept us smoking and talking round it until long after dusk and ended a day that was very well spent though it didn't get us an inch farther on our journey through the Pennine Alps.

The journey began again at 8.30 next morning, in hazy sunshine that hinted at possible rain to come. Regaining the path where it crossed the couloir higher up, we followed it on its ascending traverse across the boulder-slopes on the southern flank and rounded a steep corner on to the outer faces of the Lammenhorn. At once we were engaged with the airy traverses, scrawls beneath overhangs, and swings round exposed corners that had characterised the earlier part of the path, with the difference that the thrills were closer together. One minute you were shuffling on a ledge in a couloir, the next out on an overhanging rim where the sounds from the valley—rumble of torrent, elfin notes of post-auto horn—came suddenly up the sheer 3,000 feet under your left elbow. " *'Spectacular' too mild a word for this cliffhanger of a route,*" declares my Log.

The path went on like this for more than two hours and then began to behave more like a path, inviting the carefree stride rather than the wary sidle. Almost the last of its many intriguing fancy-bits was the familiar ledge-shuffle with perpendicular rock above and below, only this time both rock-walls were completely clothed in the glossy leaves and red flowers of alpenrose. It was very warm on the long descent towards Saas and as usual I was wearing shorts with nothing else above the belt. We met a bearded young man and a girl coming up the path and I gave them a smile and the customary "*Grüss Gott!*" Instead of responding, the bearded youth halted, wagged an admonitory finger at me, and said accusingly, "Eet ees most dangerous to go naked in the mountains!" He passed on before I could ask whether the danger was from the sun or the abrasive rock or the local Watch Committee. Beyond the scene of this encounter the path ambled down easier ground into the woods a mile or two short of Saas, forking more than once to offer alternative descents. It was here that we lost Alex.

> Crabbèd age and youth
> Cannot live together

—and youngsters under forty cannot be expected to tolerate for long the stately pace of venerable seniors. Alex had bombed on ahead as soon as the path permitted it, and when we halted for lunch under a tree at 12.30 he was still on in front. Probably, we agreed, we would find him feeding on honeydew down in Saas Fée. In fact, we were not to see him again for twenty-two hours.

Saas Fée, which we entered from 2.30 to 3 (it's hard to say precisely when you enter so long and straggling a township) impressed us instantly as a nicer place than Zermatt; and this was in spite of the dull afternoon and the grey cloud that hung on the upper rim of Saas's chief spectacle, the enormous wall of ice directly above the town on the south-west. The 14,000-foot crests of the Mischabelhörner are only three linear miles from Saas Fée and their pendant glaciers form this wall, six miles long and nearly two miles high. It's a formidable sight and contrasts most effectively with the snug little streets and shops of the town, which like Zermatt has banned automobiles from its shopping thoroughfares. Motorists drive up a road which ends in a big car-park above the northern end of the town, and walk down in five minutes to the long main street leading to a sort of central plaza dominated by a lofty church. The car-park is built like a terrace in the flank of a tree-clad hill, and the hill, we noted as we passed it, is the official camp-site of Saas Fée.

There was no sign of Alex. We paraded the streets and side-streets, lingered in the plaza, inquired at the tourist information office. No tall good-looking Englishman wearing shorts and a big pack had been seen. It was 5 o'clock and our tentative plan of camping wild beyond Saas was wiped out; also, the grey clouds had softly distilled in drizzle. There was no point in sending out a search-party—when last seen our lost sheep had been on a perfectly safe path with the first chalets in view.

Leaving a note of our identity and purpose at the tourist office, we marched damply up to the camping hill and between some dozens of tents to a fairly secluded spot among pines and there pitched the Itisa. The three of us slept in it that night without undue discomfort. Colin had been carrying the poles and Alex the fabric of the Good Companions, and it was a safe bet that the resourceful absentee would sleep dry under his bit of the tent.

This was a Sunday night, August 4th. In Saas Fée some of the shops, including the Co-op, close all day, but most of the others open for a couple of hours in the evening. This had been discovered during our perambulations in search of Alex, and it was some comfort to know that to stock up here and get away to camp farther on would have meant a mad rush. As it was, the necessary shopping was done before we turned in: one supper and one breakfast on the Saas site, and a stocking-up—the last one—for the onward journey.

The final stage, over two mountain passes and the Simplon road pass to Brig, had to be started tomorrow; preferably in company with Alex. The train we were to catch from Brig left at 8.45 p.m. on August 8th. No one hoped more sincerely than Colin that Alex would rejoin us before we reached Brig; if he didn't, Colin would be carrying three days' supplies for two men over the highest and most difficult pass of the journey.

5. SAAS FÉE TO BRIG

Saas Fée. Simeli Pass (9,916'). Bistinen Pass (7,979'). Simplon road pass (6,590'). Brig. 3½ days, 3 camps.

It was Alex who had pressed the advantages of the Simeli Pass. The easy way out from Saas on the route to Brig is by the Gebidem Pass into the Gamser Tal and out over the Bistinen Pass to the Simplon road. Both the passes are easy bridle-path crossings. The Gebidem, 7,258 feet, doesn't even rate a name on the Swiss map, and to start for it one would have to go at least twelve miles down the valley road from Saas Fée, the alternative being a pointless up-and-down along the mountain flanks above the road for nearly twice that distance. This tame ending to our journey was to no one's liking; especially, we wanted to do the last leg to Brig on foot all the way, so a bus-ride down the twelve miles of road was "out". We could get within striking-distance of the Simeli Pass in a day's walking, only one-and-a-half miles of which would be on a road, and on the other side of the pass was the head of the Gamser Tal. It was clear that this was a desirable route. It was not clear whether we would be able to cross the pass.

The Simelihorn, 10,650 feet, stands on the east side of the Saastal three miles N.N.E. of Saas Balen, lowest of the Saas villages, its ridges and those of the Böshorn forming the end wall of the narrow Gamser Tal. Alex had spotted the pass over the Simelihorn shoulder just east of the summit, a pass only 84 feet short of 10,000 with a lot of close-set contour lines on both sides. In a shop in Saas Fée I had inquired of a large man wearing a guide's badge whether good walkers with Alpine experience could get over the Simeli Pass without axes. The guide had shrugged his shoulders; if the snow was good it was possible, but if it was too hard, or ice, then axes and a rope were necessary. In other words, we might have to retreat from the Simeli, in which case there would be an epic forced-march in order to reach Brig and catch our train.

On a morning of dense but swiftly-clearing mist Colin and Jim and I dodged across the Saas car-park and down the delightful rocky path called the Kapellen-Weg, past waterfalls and ancient chapels, to Saas Grund. By the time the 40-minute descent was done and we were walking a short stretch of main road into the village the sky was clear blue and the sun pouring heat into the valley. Last night and this morning we had held lengthy debate as to the reason for Alex's absence, with no firm conclusion except that if we were to see him again it would be in Saas Grund. This small but busy place in the valley bottom can't be by-passed by travellers bound north or east and our friend was no fool. Sure enough, as we walked into the main square there was Alex, calmly ensconced on a seat. His story was soon told. It could happen to other backpacking parties so I retail it briefly here.

Alex's bombing-on of yesterday morning had taken him down a different fork of the path from the one the rest of us had followed. He had waited some time for us in Saas Fée before deciding that we must have halted for some reason and going back up his path to look for us; he must have been leaving Saas again just about when we were entering it by the other route. Of course he failed to meet us. Not realising that there was another way down, he concluded that we had either met with a delaying mishap or left the path to find a camp-site above Saas Fée. After some vain searching he had resolved that his best plan, now that evening was coming on and rain was falling, was to rig a shelter by slinging the pole-less tent from a tree and spend the night where he was, making do for supper and breakfast with such scraps of food as he had with him. Early in the morning he had got down to Saas Grund, through which place he knew we would have to pass.

We drank a litre of milk each to celebrate the reunion and set off at 10.30 after Colin had packed some of his burden into Alex's sack. A few hundred yards along the main road from the square (which was thronged with Swiss youngsters carrying rucksacks) a yellow sign pointed up a side lane on the right. This is the start of the way to the Simeli Pass; but there is no path to the pass or over it and the signposts name GSPON as the chief destination—a cluster of chalets set high up on the valley flank well beyond the point where you turn off the path for the Simeli. This point is about three hours from Saas Grund and 2,000 feet above it, where the path crosses the stream that comes down from the Mattwald Glacier under the Fletschhorn-Böshorn ridge.

We climbed slowly in the noonday heat by a sequence of zigzags always edging northward along the flank above the deepening valley. The brown Heimischgarten chalets provided a handy spout of communal water to go with lunch. While we lazed there in the sunshine looking across at our couloir camp-site of the night before last, a woman who came out of one of the chalets greeted us in good English and said the Simeli Pass was "lovely". We hoped she was right. An hour farther on the path rounded the broad corner of the Rothorn ridge and began to descend slightly into the ravine of the Mattwaldbach. To avoid this loss of height we turned up on to the open mountain-side on our right and got involved with a long and laborious climb across a glacis of large rocks; a better way, as we saw from higher up, would have been to go on down the path to

6*

the stream and come up its true right bank. However, the short cut brought us to a *bisse*, in good repair and fast-flowing, and balancing awkwardly along its outer rim we came to more level ground close above the Mattwaldbach. These *bisses* are ancient leats constructed with amazing ingenuity and toil too convey water from stream to high chalet or farm, often crossing mountainsides or sheer rock-faces where one would have said water could never be taken except in a suspended pipe. This one, led from the Mattwald torrent higher up, was still functioning perfectly though the farm it had once supplied was a deserted ruin. Its traversing channel ran a hundred feet above the little ravine of the Mattwaldbach at the place where we left it, and between the two was a charming and sheltered bowl of grass and rock with alpenrose growing all round it. Yet again, here was the perfect camp-site; and though it was only 3 o'clock the tents were pitched and tea brewed. From the tent doors the snows of the Mischabel glistened beyond a foreground of glossy alpenrose leaves. We dined outside at half-past six in warm sunshine. But by eight the mountainside was dark and chill, and the colours on the distant peaks, quickly changing from rose-pink to grey, vanished at last in a jagged monochrome of black against a sky like pale-green glass.

The frosty dew of a cold night had hardly felt the morning sun when we were away, at ten minutes past eight. 2,300 feet to climb to the pass and—fortunately—clear weather for the climb. The Simeli would be a difficult pass to find in bad weather or mist. It is not at the head of the valley, which runs up eastward, but in the ridge above it on the north. We saw no sign of a marked route and there was certainly no path. Crossing the Mattwald torrent, we mounted north-east up steeps of turf and rock, stepping over two old and waterless *bisses* and traversing east above these to locate the small lake marked on the map at 2,808 metres. This lake is the key to the upper route from this side. North-west by north from it is the pass, reached by extremely steep scrambling up knolls and buttresses of rock and boulder. Just under three hours from the camp-site, at five past eleven, we were on the rocky saddle.

Log: *"Grandest view of the whole trip from the Simeli—Dom, Täschhorn, Weisshorn etc. to westward, Oberland from Bietschhorn to Schreckhorn in the north, Great Aletsch Glacier—all crystal-clear and apparently level with us.*" There was no cold wind up there and we lounged for half-an-hour in broiling sunshine assimilating that view. Then—down.

"Down" was close on 1,000 feet of permanent snowslope, very steep indeed at the top. We tested the snow gingerly. It was the right consistency for step-kicking but the run-out of the slope was on a rim of big rocks above a further drop.

"Face in," said Alex, and once again led the way over the edge.

Doctor Johnson has the perfect description of the mountain backpacker's feelings in a situation of this sort: "He has a kind of turbulent pleasure, between fright and admiration." The Doctor was writing of walking in Dovedale, where there is no thousand-foot wall of snow suspended between huge curtains of shattered rock to descend during one's walk; it would have been nice to read—or hear—his comments if there had been. The "admiration" here was mostly for one's own boldness in starting down such a place at all, with a top-heavy pack and no axe. But any fright there might have been was concentrated in the tricky business of getting over the edge on to the snow-face, and once that was done the rest was pleasure, more or less turbulent and modified by the freezing numbness of one's left hand. Thrusting the staff deep, you kicked a downward ladder with your toes, slowly and carefully. The snow was just too soft to give you complete confidence in the steps so you pushed your left hand in for additional support. Seen between your knees, the bottom of the slope looked unconscionably far away and the slope itself nothing less than vertical. But in reality it was safe enough, and with a light rucksack and an ice-axe a moderate mountaineer would have trotted down facing outwards.

Jim and Colin, above me on the snow, thought some rocks that projected from the centre of the slope looked easier and traversed slowly across to them. When I came down to less steeply-angled snow I paused and looked up to see how they were getting on. They were moving steadily down; and my glance caught a glint of blue on the crags above them that might just possibly (I thought) be some sort of waymark.

The descent took only half-an-hour and at noon the party was relaxing on the big warm rocks that would have given us a rough welcome if we'd slipped and fallen. We had just finished agreeing that great merit had been acquired by all on this passage when Jim discovered that he was no longer carrying the poles and pegs of the Itisa. They had been in a blue plastic bag secured to the outside of his pack. The glint of blue I had seen earlier was now explained. The bare idea of climbing back up that snowslope, or two-thirds of it, daunted me; and I tried to persuade Jim that we could manage without poles and pegs for our last two nights. But Jim is not a dauntable type and back he went, a diminishing black speck on the snow and then a barely perceptible mote on the rocks, to come galumphing down again with the rescued equipment.

The snowslope on the east of the Simeli Pass is in fact a little glacier, though the one crevasse we saw was tight-lipped instead of yawning or gaping and would not have engulfed a cat. Like the Gamsa Glacier of which it was once a tributary ice-stream it has receded in the last century or two. When we went on with the descent after lunching at the foot of the glacier we were following the bed of its vanished icefall, and a very uncomfortable bed it was. An exceedingly steep declivity of crag and moraine needed close route-finding and careful placing of the feet before we came to safer walking ground 700 feet lower down. The snowy dome of the Böshorn poked up above the flanking crags on the right, we could see the green bulges of the Gamsa Glacier round the corner, and as we emerged from the side stairs of the lower couloir into the main hall, as it were, that had long ago held the thick-ribbed ice of the glacier, we saw not far below us an absolute Eden of a camp-site on a wide emerald-green plateau where there were two small blue lakes.

There was another welcome sight down there. From the plateau, which formed a sort of dais commanding the length of the Gamser Tal, a little contouring path ran east and then north high up on the flanking ridge, the last of the ridges between us and Brig; there could be little doubt that the path led to the Bistinen Pass, and with hardly any loss in height. When we looked at the map there was no doubt at all. This useful path is clearly marked there, and it was careless map-reading that had resulted in the assumption that we would have to go down into the Gamser Tal to gain the start of the path over the Bistinen.

It was 2 o'clock. But with our next—and last—pass an easy two-and-a-half miles ahead there was little point in pushing on beyond the plateau site. At its back the upper snows of the glacier pushed up towards the Böshorn, dazzling white against the blue afternoon sky. In front, beyond and above the falling trough of the Gamser Tal, the peaks and glaciers of the eastern Oberland were ranged along the horizon. There is a photo illustration to show something of the northward view from this penultimate camp-site and since it beggared description I'll leave it at that. The tents were pitched with a view to the view, so to speak, which meant being five minutes away from water; but this was another chance for the one-gallon folding plastic bucket (properly "jug", or "bottle", since it had a stopper and a handle) to prove its worth and we were soon drinking the unlimited tea which the highest, hardest, and finest of our passes deserved by way of libation.

To halt and linger at one of the "truly delectable places", to have time to idle and explore and stare again and again at a splendid prospect of mountains, was a great deal better (to my mind) than finishing the journey with long marches and a culminating dash for the train at Brig. I once heard one of the early Everest heroes, George Ingle Finch, tell a large audience of climbers that "mountaineering is not a sport—it is a way of life". Backpacking also is a way of life, a way whose chief merit is that it shows a man the best of his world. Carrying a pack x miles from A to B is merely a means to this end.

The plateau or shelf at the head of the Gamser Tal is called on the map "Ober Faulmoos", and stands at about 8,000 feet. A wall of cliffs drops from it to the valley, with a rift at their eastern end down which the glacier stream thunders to the lower levels, and a steep little path climbs beside the rift from the wild glen below. No path could be seen in the glen. So far as I know, the Gamser Tal is unknown to British mountaineers and hill-walkers; naturally enough, since it is only six miles long and gives access to no peaks of more than 10,000 or 11,000 feet except (possibly) the Fletschhorn, 13,127 feet, which is usually climbed from Saas Grund. There is no road up the valley from the Rhone—Muirhead's only mention of it speaks of an "impassable gorge"—but the map shows an exciting-looking path contouring above the gorge from Glis, a mile west of Brig, and going on up the valley to within an hour's climb of Ober Faulmoos. As I lay gazing up into the rocky hollow behind the camp, which Jim and I penetrated that evening as far as the Gamsa icefall, it seemed to me that if I were a mountaineer of humble means and skill I would find no better place than this in the whole of the Alps for camping and climbing. And I wondered whether this, perhaps, was the place A. D. Godley had in mind when he wrote his much-quoted verses and demanded nostalgically to be placed "somewhere in the Valais, 'mid the mountains west of Binn . . . With a peak or two for climbing and a glacier to explore". Certainly the glacier is accessible, and from it the whole vast complex of glaciers and ridges culminating in Fletschhorn and Lagginhorn. With equal certainty, it will be a long time before the magnificent camping-place on the Ober Faulmoos can be reached by anyone incapable of carrying a heavy load up long and difficult paths.

Next day, August 7th, we were off at 8.45 for the last of our ten Valais passes. I ought to mention that Colin firmly maintained that we crossed eleven passes, including the Simplon Pass among them; and indeed we did walk up to and down from the Simplon with only a few yards on the motor-road that crosses it. But I can no more admit the Simplon into our backpacking achievements than I can admit the plimsoll-shod hitch-hiker into the backpacking fraternity. The Bistinen Pass, though crossed by an ancient mule-track and only 7,979 feet high, was more our line of country. We gained its shallow notch easily but interestingly by the small contouring path from Ober Faulmoos, which joined the broad roughly-paved zigzags mounting from the valley bottom just below the entrance of the defile. A cold mist was blowing through the notch, and the path winding up through big rock-slabs was floored with dirty snow patches marked with the prints of sheep. The undistinguished highest point was reached at 10 o'clock. As we walked down the much less distinct path on the eastern side the mist blew clear.

Monte Leone shone like a silver helmet above the wide southward-descending valley at our feet. Up the valley wound the Simplon road from the Italian frontier ten miles away, and the sun struck a broken rhythm of flashes from the cars climbing towards the pass that led down to Brig. This time tomorrow we would be in Brig, looking at shop-windows to fill in the time before the train left for Paris. That morning I'd been telling myself that three weeks of backpacking over passes was almost more than enough for me, but now I felt an impulse to turn my back on the Simplon road and start the long journey again in reverse: up over the Simeli to Saas and the cliffhanger Hohenweg; to Zermatt—or the Grindjisee site above it—and through Täsch and St Niklaus to the Augstbord Pass and little Gruben in the Turtmanntal; Forcletta and Sorebois and Col de Torrent might all show up better from east to west, and from Arolla one might try the ladders of the Pas de Chèvres instead of the slithery Riedmatten col; and lastly the Prafleuri and Louvie cols where we had had a foretaste of the steeper snow on the Simeli. It would be good to round the corner on the Promenade des Chamois and see, down below, the green shelf of mountainside where the day and night of gloom had been followed by a morning glorious as the spring of the year—

But here we were, stepping from a side path on to the main road with successive blasts of wind from passing cars and coaches tugging at our packs. The end of the journey was very near. And I knew quite well that no reversal or repetition of it could be as satisfying as the nineteen days' travel that lay behind us.

There is no necessity (as we'd thought there might be) to follow the motor road on its 4,000-foot descent to Brig. From the broad crest of the road pass, where there are restaurants and a hotel, an obscure little path zigzags down past some chalets marked "*Lärchmatte*" on the map, heading north away from the easterly curve of the road. The start of the path was not indicated, but when found it proved to be waymarked in its upper section with the red-and-white *Bergweg* signs; and it was worth finding, for this is the centuries-old mule-track that once was the only route over the Simplon, and it is delightful. We met no one during the three-hour descent nor was there any sign of its being used. The lower part, below the ruined Taverna (shown on the map) was so overgrown that we had some trouble in flogging a way through the thickets. Just above the Taverna there were possible camping-places near the river, but the "down-urge" so compellingly expounded by D. H. Lawrence was upon my companions and they plunged on heedless of my pleas. Below the Taverna there are no places for tents. The route goes through the steep-sided upper ravine of the Tauer-bach, scenically splendid but devoid of the smallest bit of level ground. If we were to camp an hour above Brig, as we proposed to do, opportunity was fast running out, for this path climbs up to join the main road for its last three or four miles to that considerable town.

Inevitably we reached a small dam, or it may have been some other kind of waterworks, that had a motorable lane running on downhill from it. Wild raspberries on the steep banks of the lane softened the blow, but it seemed that opportunity had indeed run out—not a patch of turf, not a level place even on the slanting roadway. The lane crossed the side ravine of the Ganterbach by a new bridge; and now the massive concrete wall supporting the Simplon road was curling round the steeps close above. The ravine below the bridge offered a last faint chance of somewhere to camp and we turned down a rough track leading to a sawmill where they were just stopping work for the day. Thickets and boulders and gritty clearings bordered the fast-flowing river below the sawmill and after much searching a passable site was found among the thickets.

As with the last camps of the Oberland and Pyrenean journeys, this one was too close to civilisation to be genuinely comfortable. But it would do. There was a river to bath in and we all took a bath. There was ample Gaz for kettle-boiling and we all had a hot-water shave. The menu for supper that night was familiar from long repetition: soup and bread; bread and jam; coffee. The last square meal we had eaten sitting at a table was twenty days ago, and when we turned in there were beside the rushing Ganterbach four minds with but a single thought—of the magnificent meal we were going to eat in Brig before the train left.

Next day we came tramping down into Brig at eleven o'clock, and the journey across the Pennine Alps was over.

Log: *"Ate a superb meal in a Brig restaurant. Resultant stomach trouble lasted until we reached London. Probably a moral in that somewhere."*

SUMMARIES OF THE THREE ROUTES

Believe too little and go down despairing;
Believe too much and lose it at the end.

HILAIRE BELLOC

The summaries are intended to assist in tracing the routes on the maps. Rough compass directions are given for the same purpose. Distances may be worked out from the maps, but it should be remembered that over mountain terrain map distances are usually misleading. Place-names in capitals indicate where normal backpacking supplies can be obtained.

1. *Bernese Oberland, Montreux to Meiringen*
Maps. Landeskarte der Schweiz 1:50000, Sheets 272 (St Maurice), 263 (Wildstrubel), 273 (Montana), 264 (Jungfrau).

Montreux to BEX by train. Mountain railway from Bex to Fontannaz-Seulaz. Path and lane SE then E via Les Plans to Pont de Nant; here NE past La Vare (farm) and over *Col des Essets*, 6690'. N for ½-mile, then bear NE and E above Anzeindaz for *Pas de Cheville*, 6723'. Good descent path to Derborence (café, no bread or groceries). Waymarked path NE to *Col de la Fava*, 7639', via steep approach chimney with fixed rope. Waymarked descent NE to road mounting NW to *Col du Sanetsch*, 7330', with plain descent path to GSTEIG.

Signpost ¼-mile N along road from GSTEIG points waymarked path E over easy *Krinnen Pass*, 5446', to LAUENEN. Signpost and waymarks from Lauenen across easy *Trüttlisberg Pass*, 6686', to LENK, and similar straight-forward crossing of *Hahnenmoos Pass*, 6410', with descent path E then road NE and N to ADELBODEN. Due S up motorable lane to foot of Engstligen Falls, steep path or cable-car to Engstligen Alp above. Cross Alp SE to start of ascent path, sparse waymarks, crossing *Engstligengrat* ("Kindbetti Pass"), 8593', south of Kindbettihorn. Slight descent to narrow path across slope of Ueschinen Glacier, E, then SSE to descend Rote Kumme to Daubensee. S along W shore of lake to *Gemmi Pass*, 7620', and spectacular descent path to LEUKERBAD (shops closed on Sunday).

Ascent S by Torrenthorn path then ENE heading uphill towards Torrenthorn Hotel but bearing off SE below hotel on small path contouring slopes, no waymarks. In 3 miles path bends NE past Weisssee to *Resti Pass*, 8658'; some easy snow to cross in early August 1972. Waymarked descent path ENE then ascent NW to Kummenalp and over *Lötschen Pass*, 8825', easy snow. Upper part of descent N down glacier or rocks, care needed; then path down NNE into Gasterntal and road to KANDERSTEG.

Ascend E to Oeschinensee, taking path above N shore of lake and mounting N to Ober Bergli chalets then E to *Hohtürli Pass*, 8880'; care needed, fixed rope on descent, good path below into head of Kiental 20 mins. from STEINENBERG. Half-hour up valley from Steinenberg a path branches left (E) on true left bank of torrent then ESE to cross *Sefinen Furgge*, 8583'; care needed on ascent, easier descent E to Bogangen (farm). Thence plain path to MÜRREN and LAUTER-BRUNNEN. Signposted footpath E to WENGEN, thence up track beside railway to *Kleine Scheidegg*, 6762', with broad descent path to GRINDELWALD. Motorable lane with short-cut footpath to *Grosse Scheidegg*, 6434', and descent by broad path to Rosenlaui whence a road goes down to MEIRINGEN.

2. *Central Pyrenees, Ax-les-Thermes to Bagnères de Luchon through Andorra and Spain*

Maps. Carte de France 1:100000, Feuille XV-38 and Feuille H-24.

Spanish maps published by Editorial Alpina: Andorra, Pico d'Estats, Vall d'Aran (all 1:40000); La Maladetta, Posets (both 1:25000).

From AX-LES-THERMES 10 mins. S on Col de Puymorens road then turn left (E) for Orlu. ESE past Forges d'Orlu then S by path up Oriège river to Lac de Beys. Steep climb S from head of lake, no path, to Etang de la Grave and over *Porteille de la Grave*, 8020', care needed. Descent SE contouring to SW to join faint path on "nameless col" and follow E shore of Etang de Lanoux. At dam, take path above W side of ravine, S then WSW, to motorable lane and Porté. 1½ miles down main Puymorens road to PORTA. Cross main road to lane continuing as mule-track up Campcardos valley WSW to Portella Blanca d'Andorra, 8364'. Descent SSW for 1,800 feet then ascent W up side valley and over *Col de l'Illa*, 9025'.

NB: Port de Vall Civera, 8795', is about 1 mile S of this pass and is the better route.

Descent, in either case, to upper valley of Madriu river and plain path down to ANDORRA LA VELLA.

Road (bus) to ARINSAL. W from Arinsal on lane, then path up true left bank of Rio de Coma Pedrosa to Etang de les Truites and over *Port Vell*, 8203', into Spain; no continuous path. Descent, steep, NW then SW into valley above Tor and gorge lower down. Metalled lane to motorable road at Alins ("they have everything") and on down to main road at LLAVORSI. By car N to Bonaigua road-pass. S on mule-track up Ruda valley into Cirque de Sabouredo. Back down Ruda by path and lane to Tredos and Salardu on Bonaigua road, turning W on road to ARTIES. Due S up Val d'Arties, lane to valley-head where obscure path mounts SW to *Port de Rius*, 7686', with plainer descent to S end of Viella road tunnel. Up N on intermittent path, turning E just below Port Vell de Toro, to *Port Vell de Viella*, 8182'. Descent ENE and then N down to broad track in valley. 2 miles down this to VIELLA.

Viella to Las Bordas, main road NW, by car. Lane up SE then SSW to Guells de Joeu and Pla de l'Artiga. Path mounting W by N up Canal de Pomero to *Port de la Picade*, 8200'. Descent path W by S for ¼-mile, then branching path descending steeply SW into upper Esera valley at Plan de Estanys. Track, then road, to VENASQUE.

Road 2 miles SW to Eriste. Path NW up gorge of Aigueta de Eriste to valley-head. Pic de Posets is NW from here; steep terrain, paths obscure or non-existent. Return to VENASQUE by same route. 2 miles NNE on road, turn left across Bridge of Cuberre (Puente de Cubere) to path N and NW up Estos valley to Refugio de Estos. Due N up Valle de Gias (steep, a few cairns to mark route) to *Port d'Oo*, 9655'. NB: At rock-wall immediately under the col go left (W) for 100 yards or so and over the slightly higher scree saddle. Descent, partly over snow, needs careful route-finding; passing above W shore of Lac Glacé d'Oo, keep N until small path is found leading steeply down NE to plain track in valley bottom. Follow this down to Lac d'Oo, beyond which a populous mule-track descends to a motorable road and the village of Oo. 8 miles of road to BAGNÈRES DE LUCHON.

3. *Pennine Alps, Martigny to Brig*
Maps. Landeskarte der Schweiz 1:50000, Sheets 273 (Montana), 274 (Visp), 283 (Arolla) and 284 (Mischabel).

Train MARTIGNY to LE CHABLE, bus to VERBIER. Path up SE to Cabane de Mont Fort. Slender path ("Promenade des Chamois") rising SSW then traversing SE below Bec des Rosses, turning N at corner S of Bec Termin and NW over *Col de Louvie*, 9640', steep snow descent on E (22/7/74). Waymarked boulders E by N across Grand Desert, easy glacier, and onward to *Col de Prafleuri*, 9844'. NB: There was a difficult snow descent on the way to the Prafleuri in late July 1974. Path down scree (some snow in 1974) averaging E to Lac des Dix. S along E shore of lake on broad track and up on E side of Cheilon glacier to *Col de Riedmatten*, 9567'. Alternative route from lake: path up W side of glacier and cross the ice to the Riedmatten. Descent on populous path to AROLLA.

Bus to LES HAUDÈRES, bus to LA SAGE, short road-walk to VILLA. Waymarked path N and NE to *Col de Torrent*, 9592', descent path NE and E of Lac de Moiry. Across Moiry dam, up path N and then E to *Col de Sorebois*, 9269'. Easy descent, lower part interesting, to ZINAL. Good waymarked path starting near church climbs first E then N and E over *Col de Forcletta*, 9468', and down to GRUBEN—all supplies except Camping Gaz were available here in 1974. Good path due E up to *Augstbord Pass*, 9492'. Easy descent E for 1 hour, then waymarked route turns off to right, SE and then SW on interesting traverse, finally S down to ST NIKLAUS. Train up valley to TÄSCH. Road, then path, ESE up to Täschalp, thence by high contouring path S to Sunegga and Grindjisee. Descent by path W down Findeln glen to ZERMATT.

Train ZERMATT to ST NIKLAUS, bus to GRÄCHEN. Broad and populous path NE up to Hannig Alp (alternative, cable-car from Grächen). From *Hannig* "*Pass*", 7064', narrow Hohenweg path turns S, care needed, to SAAS FÉE. Down to SAAS GRUND by Kapellen-Weg, NE, and by signposted path towards Gspon. Where path crosses the Mattwaldbach stream strike E by N up beside stream, then N—no path or waymarks —over *Simeli Pass*, 9916', not easy, with steep permanent snowslope on descent, north side. Down NNE past Ober Faulmoos to contouring path N to *Bistinen Pass*, 7979', easy. Good descent path E and NE to Simplon road pass. From top of Simplon a waymarked path descends N past Lärchmatte and down the Tauerbach ravine, rejoining the Simplon road below Sehallberg. 1 mile down road, at Point 1233.8 on map, another short-cut path through Brei avoids all but the last half-mile of road into BRIG.

ROUTES FOR A BACKPACKING FORTNIGHT

*He travels best that knows
When to return.*

THOMAS MIDDLETON

It seems unlikely that anyone would want to journey to Alps or
Pyrenees in order to have one week's walking, but a two-week
holiday is a reasonable proposition and more convenient to
many backpackers than the periods of three and four weeks taken
by our party. The three routes described in this book can all be
shortened to give excellent journeys occupying fourteen days
or less. I have suggested below how this might be done.

Bernese Oberland
The first four sections of the Oberland route can be done as
described, but without the off-day at Adelboden, in twelve
days. This would take you from Bex to Kandersteg over eleven
passes, the highest and worthiest—the Lötschen Pass—coming
fittingly at the end of the journey. The route is summarised in
the first three paragraphs under section 1 in Appendix A. It
would mean missing out the two hardest passes of the full route;
but the two Scheidegg passes—which in spite of their fine
scenery are hackneyed and far from "wild"—would also be
lost, perhaps no great deprivation from some points of view.

Arrived at Kandersteg, you would find good rail connections
homeward via Basle or Berne. It would be worth inquiring
whether a return ticket to Bex, plus the cost of train travel
Kandersteg-Bex via the Lötschberg Tunnel, would be cheaper
than the single fares on two different rail routes.

An alternative fortnight could be planned right through to
Meiringen. Following the Oberland route from Bex as far as
Adelboden, 7 days, the Bonderkrinden Pass would be crossed
direct to Kandersteg (guidebook time 5 hours) and the route
thence to Meiringen done as described, in 6 days or possibly 5.

In this case the southern "loop" over the three passes, which I recall as the best part of the journey, would be missed out.

Pyrenees

Ax to Luchon through Andorra and Spain is a practicable journey for thirteen days if our "raids" into Sabouredo and over Port Vell de Viella are left out. On this shorter journey the difficult crossing of the Port d'Oo would also be omitted. Here are the details.

Ax-les-Thermes to Andorra la Vella, following the route summarised in the first three paragraphs of section 2 in Appendix A, 6 days.

Andorra to Llavorsi as described in the fourth paragraph, 4 days.

From Llavorsi use the bus to reach Viella, and bus or car to Las Bordas, walking up the valley southward to Pla de l'Artiga and camping there. Say 2 days.

Up the Canal de Pomero path to the Port de la Picade, 8,200 feet. (An account of the route this far, from Las Bordas, is contained in the "Viella to Venasque" section of the Pyrenees journey.) From the top of the Port de la Picade descend the path west-by-south but instead of turning steeply down to the left, south-west, keep on the higher path heading north of west. It is a plain path, and brings you in half-an-hour or less to the deep notch of the Port de Venasque, 8,116 feet. The path down into France on the north side is very steep but perfectly easy to follow, and a descent of 3,500 feet brings you to the Hospice de France on the car road to Luchon 9 miles away. There are camping-places before you reach the Hospice; with a camp here, you would reach Luchon on the fourteenth day out from Ax. Or, with an early start and transport onward from the Hospice, you could get to Luchon in one day from Pla de l'Artiga.

Pennine Alps

The journey from Martigny to Brig can be done in fourteen days if off-days and excursions are omitted; the easy Gebidem Pass would be crossed instead of the difficult Simeli, but apart from this substitution all the passes described would be crossed.

The visit to Zermatt, however, would have to be left out. This would be the itinerary:

Martigny to Arolla by the route described in the first paragraph of section 3 in Appendix A. 4 days.

Bus down to Les Haudères and up to camp above. 1 day.

Route over the three passes to Gruben, as described in second paragraph. Camp above Gruben. 3 days.

Over the Augstbord Pass to St Niklaus, bus up to Grächen, camp between Grächen and Hannig. 1 day.

The Hohenweg to Saas Fée; camp on "official" site. Walk down to Saas Grund and get bus 10 miles down valley, dismounting at Neubrück. By steep path up to Vispertimmen whence the path to the Gebidem Pass begins. Camp either below or above Vispertimmen. 2 days.

Cross the Gebidem Pass, 7258', into the Gamser Tal. Cross the Bistinen Pass and thence to the Simplon road pass and Brig by the route described in the third paragraph of section 3, Appendix A. 2 days.

This itinerary allows 13 days for the journey, or 14 if you camp short of Brig after crossing the Bistinen. It is worth noting that Muirhead's *Blue Guide* gives the time from Vispertimmen to the Simplon Pass, over both the Gebidem and the Bistinen passes, as 5 hours.

The backpacker with no spare days is well placed on the Pennine Alps route in the event of delay due to bad weather or other emergency. Every time he comes down into a sizeable valley—and he does this eight times—he is on or near a road and within an hour or two of the Rhone Valley and the railway. Supposing, for example, that for some reason he took 13 days to reach Saas Fée and was due at Brig on the day following, he could simply take the first bus right down the valley to Visp and the train for the remaining five miles to Brig.

BASIC EQUIPMENT FOR THE BACKPACKING JOURNEYS

The more a man possesses over and above what he uses, the more careworn he becomes.

GEORGE BERNARD SHAW

GENERAL EQUIPMENT (for two persons)

Tent with sewn-in groundsheet; poles and pegs
Stove and fuel (Bleuet S200 and Camping Gaz were used)
Matches
Saucepan (for soup)
Billy-can or kettle (for tea)
Candles and candle-holder (tentpole fitting)
Small torch and battery
Can-opener
30-foot line, for use as clothes-line or safeguarding rope
Small clothing-repair outfit
Small first-aid outfit
Folding plastic water-bucket
Polythene shopping-bag with handles (invaluable when "stocking up")
Maps
Compass
Toilet tissues
Dubbin

PERSONAL EQUIPMENT

Sleeping-bag (down, weight under 4 lbs)
Boots, vibram soled
Two pairs wool socks
Two pairs wool stockings
Ground insulation, inflatable or foam-rubber
Windproof cagoule and overtrousers, medium weight
Knife, fork, and soup-spoon

2 teaspoons
Mug and plate
Small towel
Toothbrush, soap, and comb

Clothing:
    Underwear
    Breeches
    Shirt, wool or cotton (not nylon)
    Lightweight jacket
    Hat, brimmed, folding

Spares, in waterproof bag:
    One change of underwear
    Pyjamas (useful as extra change)
    Shorts
    Handkerchiefs
    Light woollen sweater

*

    Passport
    Money
    Tickets
    Travellers' Cheques

Extras to taste (see G.B.S. quotation above):
    Tobacco
    Pipe
    Camera and films
    Notebook and pencil
    Woollen cap for cold camp-nights
    Camp slippers
    Travel-sickness tablets
    Staff, cut at start of journey

PACKS

Medium-size packframes with proofed nylon sacks were used by some of the party, but one framed-rucksack-type pack was used with complete success on all three journeys.

Index